CAREERS
USING
LANGUAGES

ninth edition

Edda Ostarhild

KOGAN

First published in 1982
Second edition published in 1987
Third edition published in 1988
Fourth edition published in 1989
Fifth edition published in 1991
Sixth edition published in 1993
Seventh edition published in 1996
Eighth edition published in 1998
Ninth edition published in 2002

Kogan Page Limited
120 Pentonville Road
London NI 9JN

British Library Cataloguing in Publication Data

A CIP record for this book is available from the British Library.

ISBN 0 7494 3731 6

Typeset by Jean Cussons Typesetting, Diss, Norfolk
Printed and bound in Great Britain by Clays Ltd, St Ives plc

Contents

Chamber of Commerce and Industry Examinations
Board (LCCIEB); City and Guilds of London
Institute

1 Introduction

Is this the job for you?

As the range of careers requiring some language competence is constantly increasing, ask yourself:

❏ *What interest and competence do I have in which languages?*

❏ *At what level?*
  - speaking and understanding
  - reading and writing

❏ *What would I like to do with my languages?*
  - work in the UK
  - work abroad:
    - European Union
    - other parts of Europe
    - other parts of the world

❏ *What other interests and qualifications do I have where a language could be useful?*
  For example:
  - hospitality, leisure and tourism
  - diplomacy, politics
  - industry and commerce
  - information and library services

- the public services
- interpreting
- translation
- teaching languages
- any others

❐ *Would I be prepared to study further to improve my language skills?*
- full-time
- part-time
- evening

❐ *Where would I want to do this?*
- near home
- elsewhere in the UK
- abroad where the language is spoken

❐ *Where can I get information, advice and guidance?*

❐ *How can I find out more to answer these questions?*

Read this short book as a first step.

Languages – the vital dimension in a changing job market

Career patterns are becoming increasingly fluid and 'a job for life' is being replaced by 'lifelong learning'. Increasingly, job seekers will require flexibility and mobility to be able to pursue career opportunities where and when they arise.

Career changes frequently require further training and qualifications. As a result, a flexible job market stimulates education and training, both for the individual seeking a career change and for trainers and teachers in colleges that provide training courses. Add to this the ever growing importance of continuing professional development (CPD) throughout the individual's working life and we will find that most established and aspiring linguists are involved in some form of lifelong learning.

Language capability in the career seeker's skills package will prove to be a real asset, whether in Britain, the EU or further afield. Language skills from survival level upwards can prove invaluable in many job-related and social situations – from foreign visitors coming to Britain to travelling abroad on company business or working in other parts of the EU or the rest of the world. In post-millennium Europe, language skills will increasingly become an indispensable *sine qua non*, an integral part of the new European's profile.

Therefore, school students and young people need encouragement to maintain or improve whatever language skills they acquired at GCSE or A-level and to keep up with mother tongue maintenance if English is not their native language (in Britain well over 300 languages are currently spoken in the home).

Two qualified Members of the Institute of Linguists comment on language competence and welcome the fact that change and flexibility are characteristics of this particular job market.

Case Study

Elspeth Wardrop McGlasson MIL

'First, anyone with an aptitude and fondness for languages should definitely take every opportunity to take their languages as far as possible, especially if this means living abroad.

'Second, qualifications are essential to progress. Without them, one is very limited as to employment opportunities; but they are not merely passports to better jobs. With each qualification I have taken I have felt the need for further knowledge before taking the course, and in each case felt better able to do my job afterwards.

'Third, a great advantage of pursuing a career in languages is the flexibility it offers. Some people complain about the lack of a structured career, but I would mention that this is a positive thing. Many opportunities open up, particularly when one works abroad.'

Case Study

Neville Moralee MIL *writes that when first working freelance he found that:*

'as well as being a linguist, the work called for me to act as social worker, travel guide, confidant and trouble-shooter. However, the rewards in terms of experience gained and friendships made are immeasurable.'

And still on the theme of lifelong learning, he continues:

'These jobs taught me several valuable lessons in adapting from steady work to the more precarious life of a freelance: the need to tackle new situations, often at very short notice, to adapt to the demands of the employer, to handle an irregular cashflow and to deal with the Inland Revenue, to use every opportunity to improve my linguistic competence and widen my vocabulary.'

Language competence and language needs in Britain

Careers with languages is a very wide field that continues to grow as communication across languages and cultures becomes an increasingly vital aspect of many jobs and functions in our daily lives. International marketing, insurance claims across borders, police and courts dealing with immigrants and tourists alike, jobs in travel and tourism, telecommunications, the work of international lawyers, hotel receptionists, technical personnel and secretarial and information technology (IT) staff are but a few examples.

English continues to be the most widely used language for international communication but there is also a growing preference in business for using your own language if you are the buyer. Therefore, if you want to sell, you need to use the buyer's language. To achieve this requires the willingness to learn other languages.

The widespread notion that English native speakers are poor linguists incapable of learning foreign languages is a myth. Each year many courses in Britain turn out excellent linguists. They include applied language studies degree courses at British universities, some courses leading to Higher National Diploma qualifications and courses in continuing and adult education.

Furthermore, as languages become an essential requirement for many jobs, new combinations of languages and other subjects are offered at under- and postgraduate levels including languages and business studies, law, marketing and engineering. Some courses are taught in more than one language as it is expected that students will follow all or part of their studies in a language other than English.

While to some extent the proverbial resistance of British business to other languages is still strong, there is now growing evidence of improvement in industry, which is likely to continue. There is also a growing interest in languages in Adult Education and the Open University. Ever larger numbers of mature students pursue the study of languages in this sector, both for business and pleasure, even though industry's preferred mode of training linguists continues to be in-house by language staff whom they employ.

On the other hand, there is concern about the declining interest in languages in the secondary school sector, a trend that has been evident from the early 1990s to the present day. This may have a detrimental effect on the awareness and actual language capability of the business people of the future. In 2000, French was hardest hit with a drop of 13 per cent at A-level.

The recent closure of a substantial number of departments of modern languages in the university sector completes the picture. Instead, there is now a move away from traditional language learning towards greater flexibility by opening the field to all-comers as long as they can prove competence in the required language skills at the required level.

Britain's export markets

With the exception of the United States and the Irish Republic, Britain's leading trading partners are not English speaking. Most of them are member states of the European

Union. As in past years, the USA and Germany are vying for first place, followed by France and the Netherlands, Italy and Spain, with Japan in 10th place. The EU represents the main external market for Britain's small and medium sized enterprises (SMEs), accounting for over 65 per cent of their exports. There has been virtually no change among these leading trading partners over the past few years. The fact remains that of Britain's most important export markets only two are English speaking.

It is, therefore, increasingly obvious that British business will have to raise its language capability, thereby providing excellent future prospects for linguists working in this sector of the economy. One reason why Britain is lagging behind is the seemingly justified expectation that most business partners overseas are capable of conducting their affairs in English. This assumption is on the whole correct but it is not the best way of doing business.

In the British business community there are still misapprehensions about linguists, including modern language graduates. For example, applied modern language degrees have been available since the 1960s, with students acquiring a high level of practical language skills including speaking and writing the language. Nonetheless, most employers still prefer to offer traineeships to graduates of other disciplines and provide in-house language training as and when it is required. They are not always aware of the time and cost involved in training any member of staff to a working level of language competence.

Future developments should show improved understanding of the issues and an increase in the number of companies providing training and employment prospects for linguists. Some recent developments in the UK, in Europe and globally indicate a growing realization that international communication is vital in today's world and languages are the key to it. This was also borne out by the 1999/2000 Nuffield Languages Inquiry.

2 Which languages: where and when?

General factors

'Which language should I learn?' is a question that is frequently raised and rightly so though there are no easy answers. It is important to realize that learning a language is stimulating and enjoyable but requires commitment and application. Above all, the choice you make is likely to have a bearing on your career. The decision as to which language or languages to learn, therefore, is an important one. However, the factors determining the choice are not always clear-cut.

The range of GCSEs and A-levels offered in schools and colleges may be one factor that influences the choice of language. Most schools offer one or two of the standard range of major European languages (French, German, Spanish and possibly Italian) with just a smattering of other languages like Welsh, Russian and Japanese. Therefore, most universities and colleges which depend on student intake with A-levels offer in the main the same range of languages on their courses.

At this stage, if not earlier, prospective university students of languages need to consider which languages to study, especially if they want to qualify in less commonly taught languages. Some universities offer a combination of one or two major European languages plus a less commonly taught language, for example Swedish or Swahili. Spread across the whole of Britain there is a wide range of courses and languages available. Full details of language combinations on university degree courses are in the *CRAC Directory of Higher Education* and in the *UCAS Handbook*. As the latter is updated annually, make sure you consult the latest edition (see Chapter 13).

Other determining factors are linked with personal interest and the language or languages spoken in the home. This latter aspect is important (see below).

Languages in the UK

◆ An increasing number of families in the UK speak a language other than English in their home, for example, Italian or Arabic. Much depends on how such language has been acquired and maintained. Some second generation speakers only have an oral command at survival level to communicate everyday details in familiar surroundings, especially in their family.

◆ If such speakers choose their home language as the main language for their degree or other study course, assuming there is such a course, they may soon find that after a brilliant headstart over their fellow students in the spoken language, they could well drop behind and may have to study syntax and structures as though it were a foreign language for them.

◆ It is, however, usually well worth overcoming that hurdle. If you learn the language thoroughly and possibly utilize the family or community network of contacts to practise the language you may be able to build your future career on this basis. While currently well over 300 different languages are spoken in the homes of Londoners and other major cities in Britain, there are clearly potential networks in existence that could help to further one's career. Such speakers of another language in the home are usually also familiar with the other culture. As it is increasingly recognised that communication is needed across language and culture, they have an additional advantage. (See also Chapter 4 on public service interpreting.)

♦ This rich multilingual capability is beginning to be recognized, as the growing efforts to facilitate mother tongue maintenance show, though not many of these languages, sometimes called community languages, are as yet available at GCSE and A-level.

♦ The introduction of AS-level examinations in schools has made the choice of languages at A-level easier as it leaves room for other vital subjects.

♦ Also, with greater mobility within the EU and on a global scale, native speakers of many languages are now living in most parts of the EU. As a result, a trend is beginning to indicate that employers who have particular language needs increasingly tend to give preference to native speakers of the language or languages they need. This need covers not only the major European but many other languages spoken in Asia, Africa and the Far East.

♦ Likewise, there is an increasing demand in other EU countries for linguists who are English native speakers.

♦ Language skills are undoubtedly an asset for your career. They are not easy to acquire but are easily neglected. Therefore, retain what you have learnt from your parents, speak it in the home, use it with friends and ensure that you also retain or acquire written and reading skills in the other language.

English as a world language

English is the official language used in over 70 countries and one out of five of the world's population speaks it. Over two thirds of the world's scientists read in it and in some subject areas this rises to 98 per cent. It is the main language at airports and for air-traffic control, international business and academic conferences, science, diplomacy, sport, international competitions and advertising. Three quarters of the world's mail and 85 per cent of the world's electronically stored information are in English.

Developing countries increasingly adopt English as their international language. In all EU member states (other than

Britain and the Republic of Ireland), English is now being taught as the first foreign language. Outside Britain, MBA courses, leading to the Master of Business Administration, increasingly use English for all spoken and written communication. Over 85 per cent of international organizations use English as one of their working languages. Over 90 per cent of the world's computers connected to the Internet are located in English speaking countries and over 80 per cent of home pages on the Net are in English, the next largest being German with 4.5 per cent.

The sale of education and training services to customers abroad had grown phenomenally in the past 20 years. This does not only cover teaching of English as a foreign language but also courses in other subject areas, which British universities increasingly offer to potential students abroad. The estimated value of the gross language product for English is currently US$7,815 billion compared with Japanese worth US$4,240 and German US$2,455 billion (source: Worldspeak RSA March 2001).

English as a foreign language (EFL)

There are usually at least three quarters of a million students learning English as a foreign language in Britain at any one time.

Economic rather than political factors promote the role of English as the medium of international communication and this is likely to remain the case for at least the next 25 years. A one billion increase in English speakers worldwide will become a reality by the end of the century. (see also Chapter 3 and for further information contact The British Council.)

As the EU offers its citizens free movement of labour, many European nationals may want to come to the UK to seek employment. That requires English language skills and hence the provision of EFL tuition. Evening classes for English are often oversubscribed and residential and other language schools offering courses in EFL are flourishing. In addition, around one million students come to Britain each year to join EFL courses.

Languages required in the public services (community languages)

While the major European languages, in particular French, continue to be the most widely studied in the UK (from secondary schools to universities), there has been a growing demand for a wide range of other languages. Established ethnic groups in the UK as well as recently arrived refugee groups, which vary depending on the political situation in various parts of the world, foreign students and tourists may all need to communicate with the UK authorities. This could be in a police station, in court, in a health context and when using other local government services including benefits, housing and education.

Job opportunities

Communication across language and culture is thus required in a wide range of languages. Public service interpreting has developed over the past decade to meet some of these needs. But there is also a need for bilingual workers in public health, in particular nurses, and for local government agencies, for example, social workers. In addition, local shop-keepers may cater for a particular language community, which may also require bilingual doctors, teachers and possibly policemen.

Some ethnic communities run flourishing businesses from the UK and require bilingual office workers. Others provide training in English for groups speaking a particular language. Some of these groups seek to maintain their original mother tongue in the UK for their British-born second generation. This mother tongue maintenance provides opportunities to teach some Asian and East Asian languages like Urdu or Vietnamese.

With growing mobility throughout the world, the employment sector for bilingual workers is likely to grow in size, range of languages and level of responsibility.

EU and other European languages

Another factor that could determine the choice of languages to learn or improve is their geographical spread or significance as major trading languages. The four major European languages, French, German, Italian and Spanish, are spoken in the largest countries of the EU other than the UK and represent on the whole relatively strong economies and large populations.

In addition, knowledge of Spanish opens up most of Central and South America; Portuguese is also spoken in some South American and African countries. French is needed in French-speaking Canada, and can be a useful language for communication in certain parts of central Africa and in Algeria and Tunisia. German is also spoken in Austria and parts of Belgium and Switzerland and is widely understood in Hungary, Poland, parts of Romania, Russia and parts of former Yugoslavia. The uptake of German as a foreign language is growing steadily in those countries. German is also the language of one of Britain's most important trading partners and a language which is still used in the sciences, although English has overtaken German in this area.

Other major languages

Arabic, Chinese, Japanese and Russian languages represent large populations and important trading nations, and so may offer future prospects.

Russia is currently making great efforts to bring its trading and managerial practices up to international standards. The Russians require management training, negotiating skills and knowledge of international marketing practices. All of these subject areas presuppose English language skills as they are dominated by Britain and the USA. However, the standard of English is still so little advanced in Russia that some of these training courses have to be conducted in Russian. The rare combination of management and Russian language skills could find ready employment in this area.

In China the situation is similar. China is making determined efforts to bring its economy and business practices in line with the international community. A knowledge of Chinese and TEFL (Teaching English as a Foreign Language) could be useful. For official purposes, Mandarin (Putonghua) is used rather than Cantonese, although Cantonese is the language used in the strong economies of southern China and Hong Kong. The British Council arranges for English language teaching posts in mainland China provided applicants are qualified in ELT/TEFL (see the section on ELT/TEFL in Chapter 3). A knowledge of Chinese, although desirable, is not essential.

Arabic is spoken by some 300 million people in the Arab world. There are extensive trading links and important projects which may be financed by Middle East oil. It is an area of tremendous potential. To master the Arabic script (written from right to left) is a real challenge, but the rewards could be high. An understanding of cultural differences and codes of behaviour in the Arab world is equally important.

Japanese is the language of one of the strongest world economies with extensive trading links with the UK. A knowledge of Japanese is now also increasingly useful in Britain as the number of Japanese manufacturing units grows in the UK. This is a growth sector which may require Japanese language skills from some telephonists and secretarial personnel as well as translators and interpreters.

Russian and, in particular, Arabic, Chinese and Japanese are difficult languages to learn. They require much commitment to reach a working knowledge. On the other hand, there is tremendous scope bearing in mind that Arabic is spoken in the oil-rich countries of the Middle East and Chinese (Mandarin and Cantonese) is spoken not only by well over one billion people in mainland China including Hong Kong but also in Taiwan and Singapore, where English is as yet one of the official languages. There is also a strong Chinese presence in Malaysia, and Australia is increasingly focusing on trading and cultural opportunities in the Pacific Rim which includes all these countries. Despite recent setbacks, the Tiger Economies of the Pacific Rim are expected to continue to grow.

Less commonly taught languages

The European Commission is committed to the principle of equal esteem for all languages including those spoken by minorities in the various EU countries such as Welsh, Gaelic or Catalan.

There is a wide range of less commonly taught languages the world over. Some have always held that position, such as Swedish, Finnish or Bulgarian. Others are only rarely required in the UK until they come to the forefront for political or economic reasons, as for example Albanian which only came into its own after the demise of the Soviet Union, or Slovene, Serbian and Croatian after the collapse of Yugoslavia.

There are on the whole only limited career prospects that would warrant learning such languages. However, those who have a command of such a language because it is spoken in the home or because they have a particular interest may find occasional use for their language skills, for example as an interpreter in the local community. However, knowing the language and being able to interpret or translate professionally are different skills (See also Chapter 3).

These languages will only have a limited scope for application but there will only be few who are qualified to use them, hence competition in the language market will be very low, or even non-existent, and occasional niche markets and opportunities may arise. (See also Chapter 11 for qualifications.)

Job opportunities

One such niche market came into being when the Driving Standards Agency introduced a written part into the driving test. Many drivers in Britain recognize road signs but cannot read or write English. These candidates now have to take a written test paper which is in English and may require language support (interpreting, etc) to enable them to take the written test (see Chapter 5).

Sign language

British and other forms of sign language cater for deaf people. There is now a growing awareness of the need for sign language to communicate effectively with this sector of the population. There is in particular a need for trained teachers and inter-preters of British Sign Language (see Chapter 4).

3 Specialist linguist careers

Specialist linguist careers include translators, interpreters and language teachers while for many other jobs some language competence is required or desirable in combination with other skills. Translators and interpreters are members of a profession for which the particular language skills of translating and interpreting are primary requirements. They require specialized training. Translators and interpreters are communicators across language and culture.

Translators

Speaking and writing English and another language is not enough for this job. Translators require transfer skills to convert the meaning of written material, such as correspondence, contracts, instructions, technical data, catalogues, sales literature, political documents, books and Web sites from one language into another.

In the UK professional translators are expected always to translate into their mother tongue to ensure that the translation reads like a text written in, not translated into that language. Professional bodies for translators in many countries subscribe to this rule and include it in their code of conduct, but there are notable exceptions, such as countries where the command of foreign languages is not very widespread or where very few

English native speakers with knowledge of that particular language are available.

There are, however, some translators who would argue that the command of their mother tongue has been overtaken by skills in their language of habitual use. This might, for example, apply after many years of residence in another country where they have acquired an excellent command of the language as well as a particular subject knowledge which they may need for their translation work.

Translators need to have excellent written skills in the language into which they translate because what they produce may go into print or serve as working documents or sales literature. Translators also need to have a very detailed understanding of the language from which they translate and the society in which that language is spoken. They need to ave a highly developed feel for that language and should be able to 'read between the lines' and be familiar with idiom and social customs. They communicate not only between languages but also between two cultures, and to do so they must have a first hand knowledge of both countries and their people.

In addition, professional translators require specialist subject knowledge with its own terminology. The question is whether technical literature, for example, would be best translated by engineers in that particular field with a knowledge of the other language or whether translators could and should acquire such subject knowledge. Both combinations can provide the right basis for professional translation, although in reality specialists, for example in building and construction or biochemistry, rarely have the required language and translation skills.

Case Study

Ronke Macaulay MIL has always had an interest in languages. She did a degree in business and French and, after getting a qualification in Spanish, she spent some years doing admin work while freelancing before setting up her own translation agency.

She has been a translator and interpreter in a range of languages, including several major and minor African languages. Her clients include solicitors, the law courts, local authorities and some government agencies. She herself does some translation and interpreting work in French, Spanish and Yoruba.

Ronke says that being self-employed can be excellent for people who need flexibility in their working life. The work is seldom repetitive as each document is unique, and there is a certain amount of creativity involved.

However, a translator spends many hours hunched over a computer, and constantly working on your own can be lonely. For those who also do interpreting, going out to assignments provides variety.

Salaries vary enormously depending on the clients you attract and how much work you get. Professional translators may exceptionally earn more than £50,000 per annum. As a successful translator, you can make a good living. However, when starting out, income can fluctuate and you may have to wait for considerable lengths of time to get paid for work done.

Advice to others: a high level of qualification is essential. Translating is a very demanding and challenging career, but there are many different fields. The translator can specialize in areas such as technical, scientific, legal, commercial or literary work.

Budding translators need to acquire subject knowledge. Some postgraduate translation courses cover technical translation, although the variety of technical subjects that may require translation is virtually unlimited and includes many diverse specialisms. In many cases, translators acquire or refine their subject knowledge on the job, especially as staff translators. Their translation assignments may start with general technical subjects and continue with a growing degree of specialization. (See Chapter 8 for courses and Chapter 9 for qualifications.)

The view that machine translation will soon take over most of the work traditionally performed by translators has been with us for a long time and some inroads have been made, though in any case machine translated texts need to be edited by a proficient translator. In terms of job opportunities, the choice is staff translator or freelance.

Staff translators

Staff translators may work in a team or department or on their own. As a rule, translation departments of companies or government departments are expected to solve most or all in-house language problems, except possibly foreign language correspondence which might be taken care of by an IT proficient bilingual secretary or secretarial linguist.

Translation departments are usually quite small and promotion prospects are limited. The Department of Trade and Industry has a translation unit with only six to seven staff translators. The Ministry of Defence and the Foreign and Commonwealth Office are likely to have the largest translation units in government departments.

To become head of unit would be the top of the career path for staff translators. The head's functions include allocation of assignments to staff, ensuring that standards and deadlines are met, securing additional services from freelance translators working in other languages when required and agreeing rates of pay and other contractual details. The head takes responsibility for the quality of the translation service which the unit provides. This may include vetting or double checking some or all of the work of the unit.

The number of staff translator posts is limited. Companies and government departments that require translation services may employ a small number of qualified translators, sometimes no more than one or two, whose job it is to provide in-house translation as required and to locate freelance translators in other languages as and when they are needed (for rates of pay see Chapters 4 and 5).

Freelance translators

Freelance translators usually work from home and are not part of an employment structure. Freelance translation is, therefore, often the choice of individuals who do not wish to work in organizations. Nonetheless, freelance translators have to have particular communication skills in order to deal with clients and translation agencies to secure translation assignments. They also need some administrative, financial, IT, wordprocessing and related technical skills.

Job seekers in this field, both as freelance and staff translators, encounter the problem that prospective clients or employers look for translation experience before giving a job or an assignment, but without being given a chance the budding translator cannot acquire the necessary experience. Freelance translators may, therefore, experience a slow take off in the early days of their career.

Most translators start as freelancers, gradually building up a client base and a network of agencies and other contacts, in particular other translators, usually through the relevant professional bodies. It is argued, however, that initial employment as a staff translator has its advantages in that it provides the newcomer with mentoring, guidance and an understanding of the required standard. It is important that assignments which are clearly outside a newcomer's experience should not be attempted.

Subject knowledge

Practising translators emphasise the importance of subject knowledge. Many first pursued a career in another area (insurance, electrical engineering, scientific research, etc) before becoming a freelance translator specializing in the same subject area. Some of them qualify in translation in mid-life after they discover opportunities in this field based on their specialist knowledge.

Case Study

Wendy Wingham studied languages and started her career as an insurance broker graduate trainee in London and Paris. She completed her insurance examinations and worked as an insurance broker. She subsequently used the subject knowledge and contacts from her work as a broker to secure translation work.

She says 'I feel it is essential that translators have some training in a subject other than languages. It may seem like a lot of extra work and study at the time, but it is the best way to really understand a subject and hence to translate it well. Incidentally, I never intended to become a translator.'

If you seek work as a freelance translator for companies and translation agencies, a professional approach is required at all times. This includes a clear indication of language competence and subject knowledge. Clients and employers are not as a rule interested to know whether your mother was born in Italy or whether you have access to dictionaries. The way newly qualified translators present themselves to prospective clients may be the determining factor as to whether or not they get the assignment.

Good translators are highly skilled specialists. As freelancers, they usually work on their own. In the main they are concerned with translating the meaning of particular texts into another language although they may need to discuss with clients particular aspects of the content or context of the material and in-house terminology. Variety is provided by variations in content, terminology and style. In particular, different materials may need to be rendered in different registers or styles. This requires high linguistic skills in the mother tongue.

Freelance translators today are expected to have a computer, a modem and fax and e-mail facilities as a minimum level of technical equipment. This may subsequently be expanded. Today, most translations are despatched electronically to clients and other recipients.

Networking and other job opportunities

More experienced freelance translators wishing to expand their scope may set up their own translation agency using some of their freelance colleagues or peers as freelance translators, or they may network among the membership of the professional bodies to which they belong – the Institute of Linguists, the Institute of Translation and Interpreting and the Translators Association.

Advertisements offering posts for staff translators may be found in the national and specialist press, in particular *Language International*, the Institute of Linguists' journal *The Linguist* and publications of the Institute of Translation and Interpreting.

Rates of pay

The Institute of Linguists 1999 Freelance Rates Survey for interpreters and translators and the ITI 2001 survey (see supplement in the ITI Bulletin, August/September 2001) provide details of translation and interpreting rates for a wide range of language combinations for general and specialized texts, as well as a host of other useful information for experienced and budding translators and interpreters. Rates appear to have changed little in the past few years.

Average earnings of freelance translators depend on the language combination they work in, the degree of specialization they handle and the number of hours they work per week. Any indication of approximate average earnings of freelance translators is, therefore, highly speculative but may be from £20,000 upwards. For interpreting, rates vary even more and the work is more sporadic. Freelance translators' fees are usually calculated per 1,000 words of the target text for which the computer provides the word-count. Approximate average hourly rates, where they apply, have been tentatively calculated as ranging from £24 to £28 per hour. As a rule, only the vetting or checking of finished translations by senior translators (frequently called 'proofreading' in this context) is calculated on an hourly basis.

There are still some unqualified cowboys in the field who try to undercut the qualified translators. However, in the long run, the only way to survive in this business is by establishing a reputation for quality and reliability and being well qualified. Thereby prospective clients can expect a reasonable job of work for a fair rate of pay and freelance translators can build up a client base that is likely to produce repeat business. Professional bodies for linguists are not allowed in law to recommend rates for translation. Such rates for freelance translators are, therefore, determined by market forces. They are not regulated.

In the UK, translation into English is as a rule paid at a lower rate than translation from English into another language because there are more translators in the former category. For example, translators may be paid from £55 or £60 for the translation of 1000 words of a standard text from French, German or Spanish into English. The rate for translating a standard text from English into rare or difficult languages such as Japanese may range from £150 upwards. Both rates could increase substantially for highly specialized texts. Agency fees are calculated in addition.

Rates surveys are an invaluable guide, especially for budding translators. Rates surveys may also indicate how established translators charge, if applicable, for travel time and expenses, and for rush jobs and work in unsociable hours.

In most major European countries rates for translation tend to be substantially higher than in the UK. This could be relevant for English translators who frequently find work in other parts of the EU or whose clients may be located outside the UK.

Case Study

Christine Pocock, a Fellow of the Institute of Linguists, holds the Diploma in Translation qualification (Dip Trans IoL) and runs her own language services business. Speaking from her own business experience and drawing on translation rates surveys, she summarises translators' earnings as following:

Average gross turnover of a freelancer £25,000–£30,000.

Average agency rate for experienced translator £60–£70 per 1,000 words of European languages, which means 500,000 words per annum @ £60/1,000 to achieve an income of £30,000. Average words translated daily by experienced translator 2,700 (see IoL and ITI rates surveys). This equals 185 translating days working flat out.

Plus revision/proof-reading (ca. 30 per cent more) plus research (10–20 per cent) plus admin = not many days off!

Market forces – the Internet is driving prices down, but this may be changing again.
Don't give up the day job until well established.

The Internet, globalization and localization

The Internet, globalization and localization have an effect on the language business and hence the employment of linguists, especially translators. In particular, multinational companies use the Internet to project their business to a variety of customers and markets worldwide. Their global message or products require localization so that they reflect, on the different national Web sites of the company, the language, culture and business practices of the various target markets.

As the Internet business tool grows, increasing numbers of translators are required for localization. For example, one section of one international software company has 220 employees in Dublin alone working in 40 different languages. But there are also small and medium-sized companies that are now using the Internet for their international multilingual client base. These SMEs may initially simply get their Web sites translated until they want them customized or localized for different markets.

The initial impact on multilingual Web sites appeared to be detrimental to traditional translation services. In fact, however, the Internet facilitates communication with different customers and markets and is thereby more likely to increase the volume of translation overall. This translation service can be conducted online at high speed.

French, German, Italian, Spanish, Brazilian Portuguese and Japanese are most frequently required for software localization. About 80 per cent of the source text material is in English.

In 1998 the University of Limerick developed a postgraduate course in localization and universities in the Dublin area have developed a special interest in localization issues (see Web sites www.irc.csis.ul.ie and www.slig.ie).

Translator training

Most professional translators and interpreters are graduates, often holding a specialist postgraduate qualification. They usually have a modern languages degree that today includes, as a rule, some translation. A smaller number of first degrees also cover interpreting, sometimes as a final year option.

Most language graduates who choose translating as a career will attend a one-year full-time course in translation or prepare for the Institute of Linguists Diploma in Translation (DipTrans IoL, see also Chapters 8 and 9). This latter qualification can be taken without prior course attendance, but it is a very demanding examination at professional level. A substantial number of institutions offer courses preparing for the Diploma in Translation qualification. As translating is not a regulated profession in the UK there are no mandatory qualifications. The DipTrans IoL is, however, widely recognized. The number of university diplomates having graduated after a one-year full-time course is limited. They are as a rule well regarded by prospective employers as are the holders of the DipTrans IoL. In recent years the number of professional courses in translation has increased very rapidly. (For courses, qualifications and national language standards for interpreting and translation see Chapters 8 and 9.)

Budding translators

A translator's pack is available from the Institute of Linguists that provides useful details for budding translators. The Institute of Linguists has a mutual support network of translators known as TransNet. The Institute of Translation and Interpreting (ITI) also provides information for budding translators.

Interpreters

Interpreters enable individuals or groups who do not speak each other's language to overcome the communications gap by conveying spoken messages, that is interviews, speeches, debates or political or commercial negotiations, in one or both of the languages. The legal agencies also make extensive use of interpreters.

Depending on the setting in which they work, interpreters may be required to use a number of different techniques.

Conference interpreters

Conference interpreters tend to work for large international organizations and international gatherings. They command high fees on the whole but tend to work on assignments in a freelance capacity, not necessarily full-time. The European Commission and other major international organizations may also employ staff interpreters. (See also Chapter 6.)

Because of the nature of the assignments, conference interpreters may be required to familiarize themselves at short notice with unexpected subjects, work long hours and travel frequently, for which stamina and robust health may be prerequisites. As the head of the British booth at the European Commission who is responsible for the provision of interpreting services into English said: 'A strong back is as important as good interpreting skills.'

Conference interpreting is often regarded as the most glamorous linguist occupation that can command high rates of pay. It is also very demanding and requires a particular disposition that is not easy to develop and may bear out the view that interpreters are born and not made, although specialist training is essential. The conference interpreting field has a limited capacity and is highly competitive.

Simultaneous conference interpreting

This involves interpreting one-way, from the speaker to the audience or conference. It is frequently used for speeches. While speakers present their speeches without pauses for interpreting, the interpreter speaks simultaneously in the other language. At major events, several interpreters may be required to interpret into different languages, which each member of their respective language group in the audience receives via headphones.

A good subject knowledge is essential for simultaneous interpreting. Concentration, a flexible approach, a quick mind and an unflappable disposition are also required. A detailed understanding of the context and subject matter enables good simultaneous interpreters to anticipate certain details. This helps to keep the interpreter's rendering fluent, coherent and accurate. Frequently, although not necessarily at all times, conference interpreters may receive in advance a printed copy of the speech, but there is no guarantee that the speaker will keep to it or, indeed, use it at all.

Simultaneous whispered interpreting

This is used where individuals, not the whole group, require an interpreter. The interpreter sits close to or behind the person and interprets by whispering, so as not to disturb others who are able to follow the speech in its original language. It is also used in certain interview situations.

Consecutive interpreting

The interpreter repeats in the other language sections of a speech, alternating with the speaker every 15 minutes approximately. This may require note taking to ensure that the interpreter includes all parts of the original speech. It requires a good memory, a high level of concentration and note-taking skills.

Liaison or ad hoc interpreting

In negotiations where the users of two different languages contribute to the discussion or negotiations by speaking, listening and responding, the interpreter communicates between the two sides and speaks their respective languages alternately.

Consecutive and liaison interpreting require a high level of oral language skills in the two languages as well as good comprehension skills. The interpreter's oral competence should include a clear and accurate pronunciation in both languages and the ability to grasp nuances of meaning in either language and convey them in the other language at speed.

Ad hoc interpreting is widely used in industry, for example in commercial negotiations or in the public services, including police and court interpreting. Commercial ad hoc interpreting is frequently carried out by company staff, some, surprisingly, unqualified. Their salaries depend on their position in the company, not on their interpreting skills. Some, but by no means all, receive a language allowance.

Nationally and internationally, there are considerably fewer interpreter than translator posts, except possibly in the public services (see pages 30–32).

Rates of pay

Interpreting rates have not increased substantially in recent years though some conference interpreters are high earners.

Interpreting rates vary enormously. Average earnings for a full day of consecutive or liaison interpreting may be in the region of £150 to £200 and above. Conference interpreting rates are from £300 per day upwards.

As there are substantially fewer posts and freelance assignments for interpreters compared with translators, advertisements for full-time posts are rare. (For interpreter posts within the European Commission, the United Nations and UNESCO, see Chapter 6. For freelance assignments consult the specialist press as for translators – see above.)

Interpreter training

Most interpreters are modern language graduates. Studying on a first degree course with an interpreting option is important as it enables students to acquire some basic interpreting skills and some initial experience so that they can assess whether this would be the right profession for them. This is particularly important for interpreting because it is generally understood that interpreters are born rather than trained, although training is essential.

After the degree course it would be essential to join a post-graduate interpreting course. This would usually be a one year full-time course leading to a university diploma or a course leading to the Diploma in Public Service Interpreting (DPSI) of the Institute of Linguists. The courses that lead to these qualifications in interpreting offer virtually the only opportunities in Britain to train for this profession which is not regulated and currently has no other recognized national qualification. (See also Chapter 11 for National Language Standards for interpreters and translators.)

Budding interpreters

Budding interpreters are dependent on getting assignments, usually from agencies. Some less formal ad hoc interpreting assignments may be a good preparation for more formal interpreting, although the type of technique required can be quite different (see above). It is at all times extremely inadvisable to take on assignments which are beyond the interpreter's capability and experience.

Getting sufficient initial experience to convince prospective employers or clients that you can carry out the assignment is not easy and a slow start is to be expected. Therefore, it is a general practice that at least in the initial stages interpreters also accept translation assignments, although the linguistic skills required, while very high for both professions, are nonetheless very different. Experience in one field does not ensure proficiency in the other. Likewise, it is wrong to assume that teachers or indeed anyone with a command of more than one language would as a matter of course be able to translate or interpret professionally. However, with additional training this may be possible to achieve as all specialist linguists are likely to have high language skills and should be capable of being retrained.

Public service interpreters

Public service interpreting is a relatively new profession. It includes:

- interpreting for the police, courts and other legal agencies;
- Scottish legal interpreting;
- interpreting in health care;
- local government interpreting.

It is a significant growth area for interpreters in a wide range of languages. Ethnic communities in Britain, refugees from various parts of the world, Europeans, especially from within the EU coming to work in Britain, and tourists from non-English speaking countries may all require access to the main branches of the public services. As the range of languages needed is very wide, until quite recently recourse was taken in many cases to using totally unqualified people to 'help with the language problem'.

Equal access to justice has now become mandatory. This has created a need for qualified legal interpreters and measures for training public service interpreters on a national scale have been introduced.

In 1994, the Institute of Linguists created a qualification for public service interpreters, the Diploma in Public Service Interpreting (DPSI). The National Register of Public Service Interpreters was also set up in 1994, with the aim of providing the public services throughout the UK with qualified and experienced interpreters.

To join the National Register, language skills, and in particular interpreting skills, as well as an understanding of structures, procedures and terminology in one or more of the main sectors of the public services are required. There are over 1,200 entries in the Register.

Languages in high demand in the public services include African and Asian languages, in particular languages from the Indian subcontinent, including Bengali, Gujarati, Punjabi and Urdu, and East Asian languages, including Mandarin,

Cantonese, Hakka, Thai, Malay and Tagalog. There is also an increasing demand for French, German, Greek, Portuguese and Spanish. The demand for different languages varies in different parts of Britain. The aftermath of the war in Yugoslavia created a need for interpreters with a command of various Balkan languages.

Police and court interpreters may be required at short notice. Medical and police interpreters are sometimes required for emergency cases at any time of the day or night and as a matter of extreme urgency. Many interpreters in this field, therefore, require a mobile telephone and fax machine. They may be involved in sensitive personal, legal or political issues and are expected at all times to remain impartial and to uphold the code of conduct of the National Register.

Public service interpreting is a very large field:

◆ The legal sector includes police and courts, Immigration, Customs and Excise, arbitration, the probation service, tribunals, the prison service and solicitors.
◆ The health sector requires interpreters for the treatment of individual patients, maternity hospitals and public health service.
◆ Local government may require interpreters in the provision of social services, housing and education.
◆ Other major users of public service interpreters are the benefits agencies.

Legal interpreting has given a tremendous boost to this new profession because, since the end of the year 2001, an agreement is in operation to the effect that wherever possible only public service interpreters on the National Register will be used for criminal cases in the legal system of England and Wales. An extension to other legal agencies is expected.

Public service interpreter training

Public service interpreting is a growth area for many languages as qualifications and experience are becoming prerequisites.

Some initial experience can be gained from informal inter-preting by assisting friends or relatives, but the need for profes-sional interpreters cannot be met except by qualified professionals.

Training courses in the UK, including Scotland cater in the main for mature students with some interpreting experience. Courses are usually part-time and of varying length, depending on the level of prior experience of the course participants, and prepare candidates for the DPSI. Some candidates may receive financial support. Some training is also available for course providers and tutors. Public service interpreters represent a new profession which requires, in particular, qualified speakers of the languages of ethnic minorities in Britain. (A list of training courses leading to the DPSI is available from the Institute of Linguists.)

Rates of pay

With growing recognition of the need for qualified professional interpreters in the public services, rates of pay have improved substantially, in particular for court and police interpreters. Other public service sectors which have to operate with a fixed budget are faced with the difficult choice between securing more interpreters who are paid at lower rates or paying a possibly inadequate number of qualified interpreters a fair rate for the job. Enormous progress has been made during the past 10-15 years and a continued expansion of the service based on training, qualification and improved conditions and pay is expected for this new profession.

Rates of pay vary, but some police and court interpreters receive £27 per hour during normal working hours, as do interpreters for the Metropolitan Police, and up to about £50 per hour for some unsociable hours. Many work for substan-tially lower rates of £11–£12 per hour. This is a definite growth area for the employment of specialized public service inter-preters, tutors and course providers requiring speakers of many less commonly taught languages.

Telephone interpreting

Telephone interpreting is used in a commercial and public service context (police, health, local government). Telephone interpreters communicate by telephone with individuals or groups who do not speak the same language. As telephone interpreting is usually done from home, it provides opportunities for individuals with children and others who are housebound. Telephone interpreting seeks to overcome any distance within the UK and between UK-based clients and their contacts abroad. As travel is unnecessary, considerable savings of travel costs and time can be made. As telephone interpreting is not face-to-face it has to operate without the use of body language. It makes reading between the lines and sensing fine nuances and conveying them more difficult than interpreting in a face-to-face setting.

Rates of pay

Telephone interpreters are paid for the time actually spent interpreting. Rates of pay are not particularly good and the standard of training is not always fully professional as yet. As society is increasingly dependent on technology and 'teleconferences' are becoming the order of the day, telephone interpreting is expected to be a potential growth area both within the UK and across national borders.

National Vocational Qualifications for interpreters and translators

Employers have often held the view that the British education system does not produce the kind of skills and knowledge that are required in the work place. To bridge this gap as far as languages are concerned, the National Language Standards (NLS) were created and, at professional level, Occupational Standards for Interpreting and Translation. They were finalized in 1995 and have since then been revised.

The NVQ route (National Vocational Qualifications) emphasizes the need to learn and gain experience on the job or under simulated conditions, to be validated by a recognized awarding body for the National Language Standards. Though awarding bodies for NVQs in interpreting and translation are currently not in place, aspiring translators and, where possible, interpreters, may wish to keep a record of the assignments they secure as evidence of their experience. (See also Chapter 11.).

Sign language interpreters

British Sign Language (BLS) interpreting communicates between English speakers and deaf people. BSL interpreters are, therefore, hearing people communicating with the deaf. It is a growing profession and, over the past decade, opportunities for training and assessment of sign language interpreters have been unable to keep pace with the demand for interpreters. Employment opportunities have increased as sign language interpreters are needed in a wide range of settings including support for deaf people:

◆ studying in institutions of further and higher education;
◆ in job interviews, meetings and training sessions;
◆ on visits to the doctor, optician or solicitor;
◆ at the theatre;
◆ in court.

A command of British Sign Language is also an important component for qualifications leading to other careers using BSL including:

◆ teaching deaf children and adults;
◆ social work with deaf people;
◆ residential care work with deaf people.

As BSL is, on the whole, not available as a subject in school, most students have to acquire it at a later stage.

After six years training and work experience, BSL interpreters may join the Register of BSL/English interpreters. First of all, interpreter trainees have to acquire a high level of fluency in BSL. At present there are three levels of qualification available for this. Thereafter, level 4 is required of BSL/English interpreters.

Over the last few years, the advanced BSL examination has been replaced by NVQs in British Sign Language at levels 3 and 4. NVQs in BSL, not interpreting, are also available at levels 1 and 2. Courses are usually offered by adult education and further education colleges and higher education institutions, including Heriot Watt University, Bristol and Wolverhampton. There are also privately run courses.

Having acquired a command of BSL, prospective sign language interpreters will also be required to demonstrate a good command of English and an advanced level of education and general knowledge. At present five centres in Britain offer approved programmes in BSL/English interpreting ranging from part-time modular certificate courses to those offering a postgraduate diploma in BSL/English interpreting. By the end of the year 2001 some BSL/English interpreters will have achieved the new NVQ level 4 in BSL/English interpreting. Additional specialist training will be available.

Rates of pay

Rates of pay for BSL/English interpreting range from approximately £68 to £77 for the first two hours of an assignment, and for each subsequent hour half of these amounts.

Language teachers

Language teachers require two sets of skills and knowledge. They need to be entirely familiar with the language they are teaching and need to know how to teach it. Teaching the language requires a good knowledge of syntax and grammar, even though with modern teaching methods there may be less emphasis on these because communication skills are regarded as more important. Multi-media learning and teaching facilities have also helped to enhance the language teacher's work and make language learning more effective and enjoyable.

Most language teachers in secondary schools and in further and higher education today hold a modern languages degree as well as a postgraduate teaching qualification – usually the Postgraduate Certificate in Education (PGCE). This is normally obtained after a one-year full-time course; or a teaching qualification (secondary education) in Scotland and leads to Qualified Teacher Status. School teachers usually have Qualified Teacher Status (QTS).

Language teachers in schools

Over the years, language teaching in schools has seen a number of significant changes. Technology (video, cassettes) has helped to capture the students' interest and ease the teacher's job. Exchanges and visits to and from other countries are well developed and add an important dimension to the interest in other languages and cultures. Some town twinning schemes also involve local schools.

Secondary schools in the state sector offer French as part of the National Curriculum for all 11- to 14-year-olds. A smaller number of schools offer a second foreign language, usually German or Spanish, fewer still Italian, Russian, Japanese, Welsh or other languages. Some school pupils will start learning a second foreign language after the age of 16 in the sixth form and in further education colleges or in higher education. There has been a shortage of foreign language teachers in the secondary school sector where only a small percentage of vacancies can be covered by qualified language teachers. In view of the expansion based on the National Curriculum, this shortage is likely to increase, especially for French. Therefore employment prospects are good.

In the Republic of Ireland, graduates of Irish may find teacher training an important route into teaching where Irish is the subject or the classroom medium. Every year about 15 per cent of graduates of other languages in Ireland opt for teacher training to teach languages in schools.

In the independent sector some schools offer additional European languages and also Arabic, Chinese, Japanese or Russian and some languages of the Indian subcontinent. They, therefore, offer some employment prospects for teachers with languages other than the four major European languages. This is likely to be a growth sector in terms of both uptake and range of languages on offer and well worth exploring. Terms and conditions for teachers in independent schools tend to be the same as for state schools, although independent schools are free to determine their own terms and conditions.

There is now a growing interest in introducing foreign languages into primary schools. This may well become a growth sector in the near future. Again, French is the language most likely to be offered.

The government's latest proposals may shift French tuition into younger age groups from primary school up to, though possibly not beyond, age 14.

Teacher training

Now is a good time to consider language teaching in schools as a worthwhile and secure career. The shortage of qualified teachers in some key areas, including modern languages, has prompted the Department for Education and Skills (DfES) to introduce incentives, job enhancements and flexible routes into the profession.

Initial Teacher Training (ITT) enables trainees to achieve qualified teacher status (QTS). Certain first-degree courses include modules recognized for teacher training (worth bearing in mind when choosing a first degree). Alternatively, they can opt for the Postgraduate Certificate in Education (PGCE). Recognized courses leading to this qualification for secondary school teachers may be grant funded by £6,000 for UK and EU residents who qualify.

Other routes into teaching enable trainees to work in a school earning a salary while qualifying. These flexible and varied routes include opportunities for mature students and teachers from abroad. Potential trainees and job seekers are advised to consult the Teacher Training Agency to ensure they are fully aware of all aspects and conditions so that they can select the most suitable route.

Job opportunities and salaries

Vacancies for qualified and trainee teachers can be found in the *Times Education Supplement* (TES) and the local and national press. For trainee positions also contact local schools direct. The TTA produces a contact list of people in England who may be able to offer advice on how to find a job in your area. The use of classroom assistants may facilitate the job of the teacher.

In 2001 trainee teachers could earn up to £13,000 rising to £17,000–£18,000 for newly qualified teachers. The QTS pay scale rises currently to just over £31,000, and with special additions and allowances this can increase to about £40,000 for committed and experienced classroom teachers. The head teachers' scale goes up to over £78,000. In addition, there are professional bursaries for development projects and 'golden hellos' of £4,000 for highly motivated and qualified teachers in selected subjects including modern languages (full details from the TTA).

Language teachers in higher education

The higher education sector today covers in the main universities. The university sector now consists of new and old universities because most polytechnics became universities in 1992/93. There are, however, some differences in pay and conditions. This is a very competitive area of employment.

University appointment boards seeking the appointment of lecturers in languages are most likely to shortlist recent language graduates with additional relevant experience and in particular a higher degree. Modern language degrees often combine the study of two or three languages with relevant area studies, European studies, politics or economics. Appointment boards are, therefore, not necessarily looking for applicants with a higher qualification in linguistics (which as a rule is not taught as such on undergraduate courses) but may look for applicants with a Master of Arts degree in languages and law or international marketing or a Master of Business Administration (MBA) with a language.

Most universities would expect their academic staff to undertake further study, research and publications in addition to their full-time work. Research time, an allowance of hours for these purposes, may vary from non-existent or minimal to a year's sabbatical.

Teaching languages at university may require a degree of specialization and certainly requires a high level of competence to meet the standards of language studies degree courses. University teachers are also expected to keep regular contact with the country or countries whose language they teach and to keep themselves updated on current affairs and recent events in those countries.

Salaries

For rates of pay and vacancies consult the weekly *Times Higher Education Supplement (THES)*. It is worth noting that although pay scales for university posts are negotiated by the University and College Employers Association (UCEA), universities and colleges are not bound by these in any way and tend to set their rates on an individual basis.

There are some job opportunities for part-time teachers of languages in HE. Some HE language centres also provide language training for local industries with varying language needs. A direct approach to such language centres may prove fruitful. Rates per hour average from £14 to £28 though some are as low as £10 to £12, in particular for EFL.

Language teachers in further education

As a rule there are no full-time language courses in further education colleges, but languages may be offered as options on Higher National Diplomas (HNDs), secretarial, IT and other courses in business studies. Language teachers are more likely to teach language options on a whole range of full- and part-time courses including evening classes. The level required is more likely to be post-beginners than post-A-level, although some popular HND courses may have good A-level applicants in substantial numbers, for example in the area of hospitality, leisure and tourism studies.

Because of the absence of full-time language courses, further education colleges and continuing education departments tend to employ part-time teachers. This can be a way of gaining initial teaching experience. Local colleges may also provide general and tailor-made language courses for industry with highly motivated post-experience students compared with the usual age range of 18 plus at university or 16 upwards in further education colleges.

Rates of pay and salaries

Most language teaching posts in further education colleges and adult education are part-time and paid by the hour. Hourly rates range from £14 to £25 on average and have not substantially increased durng the past few years. Teaching rates for EFL are quite low at times, from around £10 to £11. Vacancies are often filled on the basis of direct application to the language department or by personal recommendation followed by an interview.

Salaries for full-time posts start from £12,600 approximately for new contracts and can rise to £29,100 for the post of senior lecturer. Each college determines its lecturers' pay. The average salary in further education is £23,269.

Language training for industry

Companies requiring language training for their staff may ask a local college or chamber of commerce to provide tailor-made courses. Some companies employ an individual teacher to undertake in-house training on their own premises. In both cases, familiarity with modern language teaching methods is highly desirable, although some employers and a few language training providers still operate on the assumption that knowing the language means an ability to teach it. Language training in-house can be rewarding as the learners tend to be highly motivated. It may, however, have the disadvantage that multi-media teaching aids like language laboratory, video and computer aided language learning (CALL) facilities are not necessarily available in terms of either hardware or teaching materials. Irregular attendance of senior staff who may be required to travel or attend meetings is to be expected.

Knowledge and skills

In the context of foreign language training in industry, the trainer may be expected to be familiar with particular terminology, concepts and processes that are used by the company. These may be related to the employer's industry and/or to functions such as marketing or finance. A business studies and in some cases a technical or engineering background is, therefore, useful for language trainers in industry. An in-house induction programme may be essential for industrial language trainers. Depending on the company's business, languages not usually taught in educational institutions may be required, offering job opportunities for competent speakers of languages such as Arabic, Japanese and Mandarin.

Industrial learners are often highly motivated to learn the language as they are aware of the relevance of the language to their work. This, however, may also make them demanding and possibly not prepared to acquire any knowledge except what they deem to be relevant to their job.

Trainers in industry need to ensure that industrial learners make steady progress in order to keep them motivated. Misconceptions as to what learning a language actually entails also need to be tackled at the beginning so that individual learners are aware that the onus of making a success of their training lies with them. Otherwise trainees could become discontented because they had expected faster results from their learning efforts. One industrial tutor was sacked by her American employers because 'after ten training sessions we still cannot negotiate in German even though we paid you good money'.

Job opportunities

As it is recognized increasingly in the UK that communication across language and culture is an essential dimension of business, there should be good prospects for language graduates who can provide essential services as tutor, translator and interpreter or secure preferential employment as graduate trainees because they have essential language skills to offer. However, this is at present only partially the case. British businesses continue to be reluctant to face up to the need for language competence and make it part of their recruitment strategy, but awareness of that need has meantime spread throughout British industry, as the 1999/2000 Nuffield Language Inquiry highlighted.

Training of existing personnel, usually in-house, as and when the need becomes urgent, seems to be the preferred way of trying to bridge the language gap between UK companies and their trading partners abroad. There should, therefore, be plenty of scope for industrial language trainers although they may need to advertise, contact potential employers direct or work through language service providers.

Rates of pay

In the industrial sector rates of pay can be excellent. They are as a rule negotiable, but they are subject to market forces in the particular sector of industry.

The National Business Language Information Service (NatBLIS)

In 1994 the Department of Trade and Industry (DTI) launched the National Business Language Information Service (NatBLIS). It aims to provide industry with information on language trainers. In 1995 a second database listing translators and interpreters was set up. Recent graduates and up and coming freelancers may consider joining it as it might well enable them to secure assignments in their chosen field. To ensure that only qualified linguists join the database, NatBLIS encourages members of major linguist professional bodies to join the database.

Other opportunities for language tuition

Private tuition provides a taste of what language teaching entails and could be a useful first step. Some industrial clients require individual private tuition. They may have specific requirements concerning the type of language skills and terminology they want to acquire. Sixth formers and other school pupils may also seek private tuition. You would need to establish whether their curriculum also covers literature as a specialized subject, or area studies, sometimes known as 'life and civilization'.

Contacting sixth form and adult education colleges, schools in the private sector and schools offering the International Baccalaureate examinations may produce initial openings for private tuition. Thereafter, further work may well be secured by word-of-mouth recommendations if learners are satisfied. There are also a few openings for foreign language speakers, for example French or German native speakers, to teach in schools, including primary schools in the UK, which use French or German as their classroom language. In addition, specific subject knowledge may be required at secondary school level.

There are new opportunities for group teaching of retired people with time on their hands. Contact local colleges, schools and local authorities. Also look into town twinning arrangements.

Rates of pay

Rates of pay for individual tuition are by individual agreement, and for group teaching usually by agreement with the college or employer.

English language teaching

The need for English language teachers in the UK and in most parts of the world is virtually unlimited and continues to grow.

EFL is taught in many independent language schools in the UK which, if they are recognized by the British Council, may become members of the Association of Recognized English Language Services (ARELS). Job seekers in this area are advised to work for language schools who are members of ARELS and to agree contractually on terms and conditions. A number of international language schools have branches in many parts of Europe and beyond. Most of these schools require a teaching qualification for EFL (TEFL or ELT). Note that teaching English as a foreign language (TEFL) is now frequently referred to as English language teaching (ELT).

Foreign language graduates may wish to return to the country of the language they studied to maintain their language skills. This can provide a useful combination of learning and living, getting work experience abroad and improving your second language. There are tremendous opportunities in all parts of the world, although conditions are not always comparable to those in the UK. All terms and conditions should be considered very carefully and contractually agreed beforehand.

A substantial percentage of foreign language graduates earn their living at least initially through ELT. Knowing English as your mother tongue does not, however, on its own equip you to teach the language. Prospective teachers of ELT need to be aware of the communications difficulties that are likely to arise if EFL is taught at beginners' level. Such classes, that may include a variety of foreign language speakers, cannot effectively communicate with each other or the teacher. Particular teaching methods are necessary to overcome this and ensure communication from the start. These skills can be acquired on basic and more advanced ELT/TEFL courses.

English language teaching is also required in all sectors of education. In Higher Education it takes the form of English for academic purposes (EAP) to assist students from abroad. In the secondary sector it is known as teaching English as a second language (ESL) and is required in most state schools to support non-English native speakers so that they can integrate into, and benefit from, their schooling. This may be individual or group teaching. The British Association of English Language Teaching (BASELT) is their professional body. ESL and in particular EAP continue to be growth areas. In Higher Ecuation, such teachers are expected to have an English language teaching qualification and, as a rule, to have graduate status. Qualified foreign language graduates are particularly welcome in this sector.

Training in English language – ELT/TEFL

TEFL training is attractive to many job seekers especially those who have some knowledge of a language or are graduates of one or more foreign languages:

◆ There is always a demand for English language teaching in Britain and the world over.
◆ Initial training can be brief with the prospect of early employment, short-term contracts or other freelance work.
◆ Teaching English in a country whose language you know makes job and country more enjoyable and improves your language.
◆ If fees need to be covered by a loan, it is likely that they are relatively readily secured because the courses are short with earning prospects at the end.

A number of awarding bodies provide qualifications that are widely recognized though it is always advisable to check on this before enrolling. Among the best known are UCLES and RSA qualifications under the umbrella of the University of Cambridge Local Examinations Syndicate, and TESOL qualifications for teaching English for speakers of other languages, awarded by Trinity College London. The London Chamber of Commerce Examinations Board (LCCIEB) offers various certificates for teaching business English.

Training courses are widely available in the public sector. Cost and length depend on the type of qualification and the length of the course. Diploma courses usually offer 120 hours training plus study and research for students with at least two years prior teaching experience. The different certificate courses cater in the main for ELT for young learners in language schools and for overseas teachers.

Entrance requirements include two A-levels and a native or near native command of English. Many students and candidates are, however, graduates, often in modern languages, and thus understand what the acquisition of another language entails. Some employers recognize this fact and accept modern language graduates with no more than basic training in ELT.

Students have to cover their own course fees. However, in view of the massive world market for ELT/TEFL, there are good prospects for immediate employment in the UK and abroad for holders of a recognized ELT/TEFL qualification. For this reason, prospective students may wish to consider financing an ELT/TEFL course with the help of a loan, which they should be able to repay once they hold an ELT/TEFL qualification. It could serve as a passport that opens up other countries and as a useful stand-by qualification and hence an investment for the future.

The Cambridge RSA and Trinity College certificates and diplomas in ELT are recognized by the British Council. (See also Chapter 9.)

Rates of pay

In the UK rates of pay have remained static in the past few years. The average hourly rate is around £10 for ELT, in the Republic of Ireland the rate may be Ir£9-Ir£15 or less. Conditions and rates of pay for qualified EFL teachers vary considerably, both between the UK and other parts of the world and also within the UK, as much of EFL tuition is in the independent sector. Many posts are part-time and are paid at an hourly rate. However, a broad indication of earnings based on teaching EFL full-time would be around £13,000 per annum for holders of the Preparatory Certificate and £15,000-£16,000 initial annual earnings for a Diploma holder. Directors of studies and senior managers, responsible for such independent language schools, may earn in the region of £16,000–£28,000 per annum. The salary for an initial full-time university post in TEFL, based on the RSA Diploma or a PGCE, may be around £15,000, though HE institutions are free to set their own rates of pay.

For TEFL appointments in the public sector, vacancies may be found in the national press, *The Times Educational Supplement* and *The Times Higher Education Supplement*. Other TEFL posts may be advertised in specialist publications such as the *EL Gazette*.

ELT – where and how?

To come to grips with this large field of job opportunities, consider these questions:

Do you want to teach English in the UK or abroad?
To teach English (or any other subject) in a British state school, you need qualified teacher status. If you have qualified teacher status and want to teach English but do not have a degree in English, you need an additional qualification in English (see below).

Independent English language schools in the UK expect their teachers to hold a recognized ELT or TEFL certificate. There is a wide range of courses and qualifications, the shortest leading to a recognized ELT/TEFL qualification requires about a month of full-time study.

If you want to teach English abroad, a number of factors may determine your choice:

◆ you may wish to choose a country whose language you speak. This is a popular option of language graduates because it is easier to make friends and contacts there
◆ it is easier to find other jobs in the future and you can improve your language at the same time
◆ you may wish to learn the language of the country while you are teaching English

♦ you may have friends and other contacts there
♦ you may wish to stay abroad for longer and seek other work once you have a base there.

In Britain and Ireland (mainly Dublin) some EFL teaching is seasonal, mainly during the summer holidays. It is also an opportunity to try out teaching EFL to see whether it is the right choice for your longer term career.

British qualifications are recognized throughout Ireland, but in the Republic of Ireland there may be a preference for Irish rather than British teachers.

What ELT/EFL qualifications will you need?
The better qualified you are, the easier it is to get a job as an EL teacher in the UK and abroad. Basic TEFL qualifications require about 70 hours' tuition, usually in a four-week course.

The most common qualification is the Cambridge RSA Certificate in English Teaching to Adults (CELTA). Courses leading to these qualifications are externally validated by UCLES.

Another increasingly popular TEFL qualification is the Trinity College London Certificate in Teaching English to Speakers of Other Languages (TESOL).

As they are widely recognized, courses leading to these qualifications are available in many parts of the world. However, employers of EFL teachers in the USA may have different requirements which need checking in advance if you wish to teach there.

Can you teach EFL without a qualification?
You may well be able to find a job, especially if you are abroad and available at a time when there is a particularly high demand for TEFL.

Are there further job prospects for TEFL/ELT as a career?
There are various diploma qualifications for the training of the trainers to teach others how to teach English as a foreign language and get qualified. You may wish to consider such qual-

ifications at a later stage but it is important to know that you can make a career in ELT and become a course director, director of studies, or director and even owner of an English language school. The production of teaching materials may be another source of income as the production, publication and sale of ELT materials is a very large market the world over.

The ELT guide (see Chapter 13) provides comprehensive information on courses, qualifications and conditions. It is updated and published annually. Always make sure you consult the latest edition.

Job opportunities

There is a demand for English language competence the world over. ELT/TEFL is required at all levels. It is a multi-million pound business and provides employment seasonally, for a year or as a permanent career.

A major employer for teachers of EFL is the British Council, with one of the world's largest networks of English language teaching in over 50 countries. In addition, the British Council recruits staff for its own language centres abroad. Vacancies are advertised in *The Guardian* or the *EL Gazette*.

EFL is taught in the UK and the world over in independent language schools and state schools, in colleges and universities and opportunities are virtually unlimited. Job seekers are, however, advised to work only for reputable establishments and agree contractually on pay and conditions, in particular working hours and actual teaching times, that may include a number of evenings per week as well as teaching at weekends. Short EFL summer courses are held at many colleges, universities and private language schools in the UK. They are a popular way in for the budding EFL teacher, providing an opportunity to give TEFL a try.

Language service providers

Many professional linguists offering specialist services (translating, interpreting or teaching and training including EFL) find the demand for freelance work uneven and sporadic and sometimes coinciding with weekends and public holidays. Therefore, interpreters often also take on translation assignments and some translators also teach. As each specialism requires a particular expertise, such combinations of work should always be based on relevant qualifications and experience. There is no reason to assume that all language teachers could automatically double up as translators or interpreters or vice versa, but some may become competent with further training.

Some specialist linguists also use a second foreign language to translate from or to teach. Some freelancers work in teams or they network. Translation assignments may be required in more than one language. Such group collaboration can carry out the translation(s) in the additional language(s) and deliver on time. Networks of this kind are accessible through the relevant professional bodies and are usually only available to their members.

Some translators offer desk-top publishing. They may also prepare and carry out mail shots or circulars in another language, and other related multilingual secretarial services, or offer design and printing services. These are as a rule developed by individual freelancers or in collaboration as opportunities arise and the work expands. In this way, the individual freelancer may eventually run a translation agency or network with other translators, thereby being able to negotiate multi-lingual contracts or secure additional translation work from other colleagues in the network.

As translators require increasingly sophisticated equipment, a fax machine and possibly photocopying facilities, it makes good sense to maximize the use of these resources. They can get a good return from their equipment by offering general secretarial and IT services in English as well as other languages, possibly in partnership with other language specialists. There are many opportunities for using high level specialist language skills in the open market. This market is highly competitive.

Case Study

Erika Baker is a German native speaker resident in the UK: 'I first read the original book on Careers using Languages at a time when I found myself trapped in a job I didn't much enjoy, but without any clear idea of where I wanted to go, other than "wanting to use my languages".' In 1985 she studied in Japan for a year and gained a Japanese language qualification comparable to A-level. She then worked in energy research for a Japanese company in London with responsibility for German speaking countries in Europe involving English into German translation and interpreting and extensive use of Japanese.

Having gained the Institute of Linguist's Diploma in Translation and the ELIC Diploma, she has been working freelance since 1994 providing 'anything that adds value to "mere" translations'. She provides the kind of service 'a customer who does not know anything about "abroad" needs to know to succeed'. Her clients include small and medium sized service providers – manufacturers, builders, plumbers, etc, who are trying to establish themselves in Germany. She networks with others in the field to provide back-up support and additional advice and information.

She works from home and continues to expand her work into a fully-fledged language services company.

Rates of pay

Earnings vary enormously and depend on quality and the size of the client base that has been built up over time. Few individuals earn more than £50,000 per annum. Earnings are invariably higher in other European countries, where English native speakers translating into English can often command high fees.

Language examiners

These represent another group of language service providers.

Many thousand candidates take language examinations every year, including A-levels and GCSEs. The latter cover not only examinations in the four major European languages, but also Arabic, Chinese, Japanese, Punjabi and Urdu. The International Baccalaureate examines a range of world languages at levels above GCSE and A-level.

In addition, there are a number of external examinations boards for languages including the Oxford Cambridge RSA (OCR), Trinity College London, the London Chamber of Commerce (LCCI/EB) and City and Guilds. They concentrate in the main on the lower levels (post-beginners to A-level equivalent).

The Institute of Linguists offers a number of examinations and language qualifications to degree equivalent and postgraduate levels. These examinations can be provided in a wide range of less commonly taught languages. In addition, the Institute's Language Services Unit provides tailor-made tests and assessment schemes in any language and at any level as required by individual clients. In all, over 150 languages can be assessed by the Institute of Linguists.

All these boards require examiners and setters. Setters provide the test papers and examiners mark the scripts. Oral examiners are frequently required by examination centres, as well as interlocutors (for dialogues in a foreign language and English). Most of this work is done by freelance linguists who may need training to ensure that they know the standard of the examinations. At the higher levels, well-qualified and experienced examiners are required. Setting of papers and script marking are usually done from home. The work is seasonal and examiners do not usually work full-time. Language examining may provide welcome additional income and interest.

4

Languages in industry and commerce

Industry and commerce including banking, insurance, shipping and telecommunications represent a very wide international field. The need for communication with speakers of other languages is global and includes Britain's European trading partners as much as other parts of the world where European languages are not widely used. Today it is no longer good business practice to expect all transactions and social contacts to be conducted in English. This applies to East Asia and increasingly to parts of the Indian subcontinent and Malaysia and many other parts of the world.

There is a need for most languages somewhere in industry and commerce. There is a need for different language skills and for such skills at different levels. It is increasingly recognized that spoken skills, the ability to conduct a conversation, are the most important language skills, from managing director to receptionist.

The skills required

The following five common factors have been identified:

◆ Management, especially marketing, and technical and secretarial levels need languages.
◆ The higher the level of management, the less specialized is

the vocabulary that is required, but at the same time language skills in general terms are more important.

◆ Technical and secretarial personnel often require particular knowledge and specialized terminology.

◆ The most important language skills for all levels of management and technical and secretarial personnel are oral and listening skills, to speak and to understand what others are saying.

◆ Marketing together with top level management are the areas with the most widespread need for a command of foreign languages.

Management, marketing and exports

Virtually all businesses today and certainly large companies have at least an occasional need for foreign languages.

Languages open up vital sources of business information and also enable UK companies to provide information to potential markets and customers abroad. Skills in English and in other languages are required in many negotiations, in deals, offers, agreements and contracts. Sales literature needs to be directed at other markets in their language in a way that makes such markets receptive to the contents, the message and the product.

Exporting companies require such language skills throughout the transaction, from the initial offer in their sales literature to subsequent correspondence, telephone calls and negotiations leading to an agreement, which is then confirmed in a contract. This is followed by documents accompanying the goods to be exported, including user instructions or technical data. Subsequently there will be invoices, their confirmation and settlement, requiring banking services in the UK and abroad which in turn require skills in different languages.

Such a process requires language skills for the exporting company at managerial level, backed by the skills of a secretarial linguist and possibly a bilingual receptionist or telephonist. Of course, most of the trading partners abroad, when dealing with

British companies, could and do conduct such business or parts of it in English. However, it has become increasingly standard practice to expect the seller to conduct at least part of the transaction in the buyer's language.

The ability to hold a conversation with your business partners abroad, even if only in a social context, is usually very welcome and contributes to a successful business partnership. It helps in the successful conclusion of transactions between business partners in different countries, be that within the European Union or elsewhere.

Understanding another language is closely linked with gaining access to the culture and society where the language is spoken. Understanding of a culture plays an important role in marketing, advertising and selling. No business can be entirely successful unless it knows its markets and its customers and speaks their language.

Salaries and earnings

Rates of pay for these jobs are determined by the position the individual holds in the company, although language skills may be the determining factor in securing the appointment and may make the postholder particularly valuable to the employer and to the job market in general.

Job opportunities

This growing need for language capability is reflected by the employment agencies in the UK. An increasing number of such organizations cater specifically for bilingual or multilingual job seekers. Consult the national press for vacancies.

On the other hand, vacancies for international marketing and similar posts do not necessarily stipulate another language even though it may be the determining factor to getting the job. Consult the national and regional press and company Web sites. Try your luck!

Technical personnel

Technical personnel often require an understanding of essential terminology in another language. Sometimes specialist reading skills are required to access technical information (for example, in tenders and other specifications). Oral skills may also be necessary to communicate with technical personnel and other specialists abroad. For more specialized tasks, technical personnel may require the services of a translator.

Secretarial linguists

Companies working in the international field may require general correspondence in other languages. In addition, they receive letters and other material which are not in English. Secretarial linguists and bilingual secretaries have the skills necessary to compose letters in the other language and translate, for in-house use, incoming letters into English. They may be expected to translate other printed matter, although sales literature and advertising copy should be handled by specialist translators or speakers of the other language who are experts in the field and who can also take cultural differences into account and use idiom effectively.

Secretarial linguists may also need to handle telephone calls in another language or translate fax messages into English. Occasionally, they may be expected to liaise between the two languages as ad hoc interpreters if visitors who do not have a fluent command of spoken English seek to conduct discussions or negotiations in the UK.

Secretarial linguists may also require good keyboard and other secretarial skills. They are likely to work for one or two directors or managers. Bilingual secretaries may be required to provide a more broad-based in-house language service and are likely to communicate in the foreign language, whether spoken or written. For technical or other documentation, however, the secretarial linguist may have to locate, evaluate and commission freelance translators or the services of a translation agency.

Secretarial linguist training

OCR and LCCIEB provide vocational or business oriented language qualifications. Language tuition on these courses places an emphasis on commercial terminology, usually in French, German, Spanish and sometimes Italian, although a few courses now also offer rarer language combinations. There have been significant changes in training and qualifications for secretarial linguists (see Chapter 10).

Salaries

Established secretarial linguists working full-time including postgraduate secretarial linguists may hold highly responsible jobs with good prospects of increased earnings. Some secretarial linguists' jobs expand into international administrators or co-ordinators, with salaries in the region of £30,000–£35,000 or above.

Finance, banking and insurance

There are many posts in the world of finance and insurance that require language skills, although locating these posts may require some effort. The reason here is that the need for language skills for a particular post may not become apparent until the postholder has been established in the job for a considerable time. For example, an opening may arise in Germany in a branch of a major UK bank. Only highly experienced individuals in the field, possibly from within the bank itself, would qualify providing they also have the required language skills. However, banks also have some openings abroad for their more junior personnel if they have the necessary language skills.

High level oral skills in other languages are frequently a great asset for dealers in the stock markets in the UK and abroad and commodity markets (where sugar, metal, etc are bought and sold) have a need for oral skills in a range of languages.

The insurance business works increasingly on an international scale where languages are an asset and for some posts they may be essential. Again, the need for language skills may not be apparent when graduate trainees take up their first post, but as they progress, new opportunities in the international field may arise that require particular language skills.

Potential high-flyers should be aware that some opportunities in industry and commerce only arise if the need for language skills can be met and should at least develop good oral skills and maintain them. Insurance companies are increasingly dealing with clients and claims across national borders involving communication in other languages.

Receptionists and telephonists

As international business expands, receptionists and telephonists are increasingly likely to encounter non-English speaking customers or clients. Some language ability may be needed and would help to clinch such jobs.

Receptionists and telephonists may require quite limited language skills in a general social context (to greet and welcome) and to identify the visitors' or callers' needs so they may be passed on to the relevant senior staff or management, or to a competent linguist within the company to take over. Britain is currently lagging behind other major European countries in these language skills.

Travel, tourism, leisure and hospitality

The travel, tourism, leisure and hospitality industry is today a major sector of the British economy. The industry is expected to grow rapidly in the next few years. A substantial number of visitors to the UK do not speak English and are dependent on their languages being spoken by the British work force in the tourism and leisure sector.

For most occupations in the tourism and leisure industry language skills are desirable. For those who have direct dealings with visitors, for example hotel and catering managers, front-of-house personnel, conference organizers, all four language skills are essential. Most other personnel in tourism and leisure only require speaking and listening skills in the other language and frequently only to GCSE or A-level equivalent at the most.

Job opportunities

The many young people in the UK today who speak another language at home and have, therefore, good spoken and listening skills may well wish to explore the tourism and leisure industry for jobs where their language skills would provide good prospects of success. Such jobs could be seasonal, such as during holiday periods from their studies. But there are also permanent posts and prospects for promotion in this ever growing sector of employment.

Britain receives millions of visitors from non-English speaking countries every year, and yet less than 10 per cent of the firms in this field have a language policy.

Hotels, many belonging to international chains, market their services internationally, that is hotel, restaurant and other catering services plus conference and leisure facilities. They may require marketing personnel with language skills. Hotel bookings may be made in foreign languages, by telephone, fax, e-mail or letter, requiring secretarial linguist skills of the front-of-house hotel staff. Hotel receptionists and telephonists need at least some basic oral language skills as not all hotel guests and conference participants will be proficient in English.

Tour operators, offering tours to all parts of the world, require couriers, guides and other personnel with oral language skills working in the UK and at the various tour destinations. Some of these jobs are seasonal and may provide welcome opportunities to work abroad for short periods of time.

Travel agents may have similar requirements.

International airlines require in-flight and ground personnel with oral language skills, although the international language of airports is English.

Airlines have realized that the ability of their cabin staff to communicate with passengers in their respective languages adds an important dimension to the airline's customer service. They seek to ensure, therefore, that cabin crews have at least one additional language or they may undergo free training. There are several levels of competence, at the basic level, the exchange of common courtesies and essential safety information, beyond that training is offered to different levels of competence.

The ability to communicate with passengers in their language is so important to the airlines that the language competence of cabin staff also plays a major part in the general prospects for promotion. Applicants who have a command of another language have, therefore, a threefold advantage: they are more likely to get the job, they are likely to get a language allowance right away and, because they know what learning a language entails, they are likely to use the airline's language programme to qualify in additional languages and secure additional pay and promotion prospects.

Events relating to the September 11 2001 crisis have seriously affected tourism and travel and in particular international airlines. Some went out of business; others had to make drastic cuts, which have particularly affected customer services including language policies. With time, these services are likely to be revived though they may take a different form.

Salaries and rates of pay

Language competence, especially oral in more than one additional language, is regarded as a major factor in determining salary levels. Language allowances vary but may range from £100 per annum to £500 per level and language. This enables some individuals to increase their earnings by £1000 and more per annum.

Case Study

Matthew Major worked for British Midlands Airways, starting as a member of the cabin staff. He decided to utilize the airline's language training programme to the full and became the only person company-wide to speak 10 languages to a basic level including Czech, Danish, Dutch/Flemish, Gaelic/Irish, German, Italian, Norwegian and Spanish. He took French at the highest level and decided to take this language training further and also bring German up to the highest level. His newly acquired language competence enhanced his promotion prospects and he became flight supervisor at London Heathrow with a substantially increased salary. He regards languages as vital for airline customer services.

The Channel Tunnel operators Eurostar introduced a distinct language policy for all their personnel. They recruit staff with or without foreign language skills, then train all staff in French, to different levels of competence depending on which language skills their particular functions require. Even graduates in French undergo French language training to acquire specialist terminology and improve fluency. This positive foreign language policy provides employment openings for French speakers at different levels.

The majority of jobs in travel and tourism require oral competence though not at degree level. It is an area suitable for many career seekers with A-level or good oral language skills at GCSE level or those who speak another language at home and have fluency, although possibly limited application and vocabulary. Some HND courses in travel and tourism offer the major European languages as an option.

Tourist guides need to be able to combine fluent spoken language skills with geographical and historical knowledge of the cities, buildings and museums where they operate. They require cultural knowledge as well as presentation skills, on foot, on site or on a coach. Additional study at home is essential. On application, all prospective guides take a short compulsory language test. Some guides specialize, for example, in fine art, Constable country or local history. Adequately qualified tourist guides may be asked to contribute to the creation of guidebooks or brochures or translate such material. Tourism has been a growth area for many years though there has been a set-back since the events of September 11.

Blue badge guides: Successful applicants qualify as registered guides and are awarded the Blue Badge, which is recognized internationally. Blue Badge guides are self-employed and take on freelance work. This is a new profession with its own emerging professional body, the Tourist Guiding Foundation.

Rates of pay

Fees may vary according to market forces and competence. In London, guides working in any language other than English will expect to earn a minimum of £161 for a full day's work and £102 per half day.

Some tourist information centres on the south coast have introduced a staff exchange with their French counterparts on the other side of the Channel. Tourism and leisure also includes international sports facilities and events, exhibitions and venues for international gatherings, ferries and pleasure boats as well as youth hostels.

There are a number of professional bodies in the tourism and leisure industry who may provide information and literature for career seekers (see Chapters 12 and 13).

5   The professions and other careers using languages

Languages and the professions

The professions, like industry, are increasingly working across national borders, languages and cultures. With ever growing freedom of movement and employment within the EU and Europe as a whole, there is an ever closer link between the affairs of the countries of Europe in commercial as much as professional terms. Jobs include:

◆ lawyers
◆ architects
◆ scientists
◆ engineers
◆ information officers and librarians
◆ accountants
◆ medical personnel
◆ public service workers

There is now a need for skills and knowledge combinations, for example in law and languages or accountancy and languages. In addition, consortia of architects, surveyors and building contractors working across national borders and cultures require language skills at various levels to communicate with a multilingual workforce. Some international law firms employ language specialists, usually translators, secretarial linguists or bilingual legal secretaries. International building firms and architects may employ project co-ordinators for general planning and communication across national borders and on site. Accountants employed by companies with international interests may be required to work on assignments abroad, for which language skills may be essential or desirable. The work of computer companies and consultants of all kinds is no longer confined within national borders.

While language skills were originally of secondary significance, they are increasingly regarded as essential, at least for some members of these professions. Such skills may be bought in by employing the services of others if the professional does not have the necessary language skills. The language skills needs in the professions fall into two groups – the professionals themselves and ancillary jobs including international co-ordinators, events organizers, secretarial linguists and bi- or multilingual receptionists and telephonists. All need oral skills, although some members of these professions may also require reading and writing skills in another language.

The need for language skills in the professions is increasingly reflected in new subject combinations on degree courses including languages. It is also reflected in the university-based institution-wide language programme (IWLP) which is designed to provide access to foreign language learning for all undergraduates regardless of the main subject they study.

Job opportunities

Lawyers within the EU, for example, may deal with cases involving more than one language. They may, therefore, require bilingual secretaries, translators or interpreters (see also Chapter 3). They may also need language skills themselves.

Architects may work in an international consortium or on international projects. They may require liaison personnel to bridge the language gap. They and their building contractors may also require multilingual site managers, supervisors and engineers to communicate with the workforce on site in the UK and abroad.

Scientists and *engineers* increasingly work across borders and continents. Their language needs have been recognized by their own professional bodies, which have their own language support schemes. They are currently seeking to include languages into their continuing professional development schemes. Technical personnel working at all levels (from the drawing board to the building site) may work on assignments anywhere in the EU or beyond, and a knowledge of other languages, from survival level in the spoken language to reading instructions and technical data, may be essential.

Information officers and *librarians* may be expected to scan specialist literature in foreign languages for particular information purposes or assignments. This work requires good reading skills in the other language or languages. They may also need to abstract information translated from the English source material. This requires written skills in the other language or languages.

Fast developing areas in science, technology and industry are dependent on a regular supply of such information, often through the specialist press, where information officers as well as translators may be employed. The use of the Internet for information purposes continues to expand and is likely to stimulate the demand for multilingual writing and reading skills. (See also under journalism, publicity and the media below.)

Accountants and *financial consultants* often work in the context of international projects or with clients within the EU or beyond and may require secretarial linguist skills to communicate with their opposite numbers abroad. At times they may use a translator or interpreter.

Medical personnel, doctors, nurses, hospital staff, often encounter non-English speakers, sometimes in emergencies. They may themselves be bilingual and, therefore, able to communicate in a particular ethnic language or they may use interpreters as required (see also Chapter 3).

Bilingual public service workers are required in education, housing and other local government departments as well as the benefits agencies. They may have undergone their own professional training, for example as social workers, but they may also be required to speak a language other than English, for example, Arabic, Bengali, Cantonese, Gujarati, Punjabi and some of the African languages, languages which are frequently spoken in the homes of UK citizens and residents.

Members of ethnic communities in the UK require such bilingual personnel in the social services, the National Health Service, counselling, Citizens Advice Bureaux and other advisory services. The Refugee Councils, the Council for Racial Equality and their networks within the local authorities in the UK all require bilingual workers to communicate with non-English speaking members of their community. It is an area providing employment for members of ethnic communities in the UK.

The Driving Standards Agency (DSA): Since the introduction of a theory test, candidates for the driving test need to know sufficient English to understand the written test. For candidates without English reading skills, the DSA provides language services. At any one time, the DSA provides a voice-over service in the 20 languages required most frequently by candidates with an inadequate knowledge of English.

These languages change from time to time according to demand. Candidates requiring language support are provided with names of selected translators. Measures are in place to prevent collusion. For some time now this has been a growth area for job seekers, usually on an assignment basis, in a variety of community languages including Polish, Portuguese and Welsh.

Salaries

Salaries have been modest and until recently virtually no recognition was given to the bilingual capability of such employees in the public services. However, there is growing recognition that bilingual workers in the public services meet an urgent communications need of many non-English speaking UK citizens and residents. With an increasing uptake of qualifications and growing professionalism, rates of pay are gradually improving (see also Chapter 11).

The Civil Service

The Civil Service requires linguists in a variety of posts, including translators, interpreters and information officers. In some branches of the Civil Service, language skills are recognized by payment of a foreign language allowance.

Job opportunities

A number of government departments employ staff translators, including the Ministry of Defence and the Departments of Transport, the Environment and Trade and Industry with its new section Trade Partners UK. Their staff translators always translate into English. Translation work from English into other languages is usually done out-of-house by freelance translators. The Foreign and Commonwealth Office employs a small number of staff linguists to provide translation, information services and language training for Foreign Office personnel. Interpreters are usually freelance.

Qualifications required of Civil Service linguists are as a rule a good second class Honours degree and usually a postgraduate diploma or relevant experience. The basic requirement is competence in two foreign languages. All applicants then take language tests in open competition. British nationality of the applicant is a precondition which may also apply to his or her parents and needs to be clarified in advance.

Rates of pay and conditions

There are three grades for civil service staff translators, ranging from assistant to head of unit. The standard salary range used to be around £14,000 to £28,000. However, government departments are now free to set their own rates of pay. For example, at the DTI the range is approximately £19,000 to £24,000 rising to £25,000 and above for senior translation advisers. They may vary depending on supply and demand and departments are free to increase rates of pay if necessary. Job vacancies are usually handled by CAPITA and publicized on the Internet www.capitaras.co.uk). Information is also available from the various government departments. Depending on security requirements, government departments may have nationality and residency conditions.

The Government Communications Headquarters (GCHQ) and the Joint Technical Language Services (JTLS)

GCHQ/JTLS in Cheltenham is a branch of the Civil Service employing language graduates as well as other professionals. It is the government's headquarters for gathering and monitoring news and information from abroad for national security and related purposes.

GCHQ and JTLS serve the British government's defence and intelligence needs. Linguists working at GCHQ are required to monitor a wide range of telecommunications, consequently highly developed listening skills in other languages are necessary. The linguists working at Cheltenham also translate or transcribe foreign language material which is often of a highly technical nature and undertake research studies by tracking down and recording information on specific topics.

Selection procedures include a competitive language test. At times, applicants offering Arabic, Chinese, Farsi (modern Persian), Japanese and Russian are particularly welcome but, language requirements may change depending on the political circumstances at the time. Other recruits may be expected to acquire an additional language from scratch and are offered intensive training. In the course of their career with GCHQ they may be required at various stages to learn further languages, possibly spending a year or more abroad. There is ample scope for promotion and training is provided within a well defined careers structure.

As well as working for GCHQ, linguists may be employed in the JTLS, which provides linguistic support for other government departments. Linguists working with JTLS enjoy the same opportunities for career progression as GCHQ staff.

Particular conditions apply for the security and intelligence work at GCHQ/JTLS. They specify that applicants must be British citizens or, if you hold dual nationality, one component must be British and you will normally be required to give up any non-British component. (See www.gchq.gov.uk for further details).

Salaries

The standard salary range for a new entrant linguist at GCHQ/JTLS is currently approximately £17,600 to £22,000 with prospects of moving into higher pay ranges depending on skills and experience. Through time, you may be eligible for promotion and move into the next pay range of approximately £20,500 to £25,600 or higher plus performance-related pay.

The Diplomatic Service

The Diplomatic Service staff policy includes the employment of graduate linguists. These posts are much sought after. Even though the Diplomatic Service sets very high standards for its recruitment, there is usually no problem in securing excellent linguists because of the large number of applicants in this competitive area. Recruitment is based on selection followed by competitive language tests. Once in position, linguists may be expected to undergo intensive training in an additional language. They could be posted anywhere in the world and may change location every two to three years. They are expected to represent their country at all times. Before being posted abroad, members of the Diplomatic Service Overseas may receive about 18 months' intensive tuition in the languages required. They and their families also have to meet various nationality requirements which applicants should clarify in advance. (For more details see 'On Her Majesty's Service' (2002) in the Institute of Linguists' journal *The Linguist*, 41(**1**), pp 23–25.)

Patent Agents, Patent Examiners and the Patent Office

Patent Agents obtain patent protection for inventions within Europe where they deal with the European Patent Offices in The Hague, Berlin or Munich, which use English, French and German. A command of French and German is, therefore, in particular demand. They carry out searches to verify that a particular invention is genuine and describe how it works, or they seek protection for registered designs and trade marks. They then file applications and negotiate with the Patent Office.

Patent examiners work in the same field. They examine incoming patent applications for the Patent Office. They need the same combination of qualifications and skills in engineering, science or technology and languages.

Patent agents and patent examiners require language skills to conduct correspondence, negotiate and frequently translate. They also need good reading skills to access complex material in another language. Many employ freelance translators as necessary. Again, French and German are in demand but also other languages.

The Patent Office, the government department dealing with patent applications, recruits primarily graduate scientists and engineers. Language competence, in particular in French, German and also Japanese, is an added bonus. If competence in a particular language is required, in-house tuition is provided, usually in French and German. The Patent Office also works closely with the World Intellectual Property Organization in Geneva where English, French and German are the working languages and linguists are recruited as the need arises. Freelance interpreters and translators who are fluent and competent in at least two, and able to work in the third of these, languages may work for this organization.

Salaries and earnings

In view of the highly technical nature of the work, contracts and commissions are negotiable. Similar conditions and rates of pay apply to all staff translators in government departments. However, some departments have a more commercial dimension (for example the DTI). Others need to take account of the highly specialized or technical nature of their translation work (for example the Patent Office). As a result, there is some room to negotiate rates of pay within some sections of the Civil Service.

Journalism and the media

The press requires linguists for a variety of functions. The national press receives its international news and other information from many sources. They may, therefore, use translators as required but foreign news is usually received in English from Reuters and other press agencies who are, of course, themselves in the media business and use translators on a regular basis.

Job opportunities

Depending on particular specialisms, most journalists and reporters on location abroad could well use language skills and many of them do. They may, in fact, be able to establish themselves as journalists precisely because of their knowledge of a particular language, culture and country from where they secure topical or significant news items and reports. Like translators they need good writing skills.

Other media, in particular television and radio, may operate foreign language services for which they require as a rule mother tongue speakers as newscasters and programme presenters. They also employ translators or use newscasters to translate news and other material from English into the required languages. The BBC World Service employs many native speakers of other languages who also have an excellent command of English. Jobs are much sought after and as a result it is a highly competitive area.

The *BBC's monitoring unit* in Caversham, which monitors broadcasting stations abroad, requires linguists with a range of languages spoken the world over. They monitor and write up or summarize in English what they hear. Occasionally they produce a newsflash if they are the first to hear over the air a major news item from abroad. Good listening comprehension in such a language is the major prerequisite. Again, this is a highly competitive area. The demand for any particular language may well depend on the international political situation of the day. Similar language skills are also required at GCHQ in Cheltenham (see the Civil Service).

Publicity and advertising

Publicity and advertising have always had a certain glamour. Ambitious young linguists planning their careers tend to find this area particularly attractive. However, copy writers abroad or in the UK who are native speakers of the required language tend to be used because they are usually best able to produce advertising copy in languages other than English. They know how to sell to a potential foreign market, they know the cultural differences and have the ability to create, not translate, the right advertising material for particular consumer groups abroad. Native speakers of other languages with a flair for writing and selling may find this an interesting although highly competitive field of employment with limited openings. Some creative translators recreate advertising copy rather than translate it.

Careers requiring limited language competence

Language skills can be acquired in many different ways. Apart from degrees with languages and postgraduate courses for interpreters and translators, adult and continuing education centres provide a wide range of language classes, mainly in the evening. The biggest uptake is for beginners' classes every year, although with commitment and staying power, individuals may reach a good working knowledge, at least in spoken communication. Some keep up their school French or German by distance learning, using the Internet or self-access study, usually with the help of a local college or language centre. First language teaching jobs may be on offer for newcomers to this field.

Job opportunities

As ever more tourists travel the world over and require services, there are increasing opportunities to use foreign language communication skills in employment from hotel receptionists to catering and restaurant staff and shop assistants in the fashion, cosmetics, souvenirs and antiques trades. Telephonists, office workers, hospital staff at all levels and personnel in entertainment, travel agencies, railways, airports, both ground and in-flight staff, may need foreign languages, in particular spoken skills. Some police forces in the UK now look for new recruits with language skills – for work in the local community or with tourists and workers from abroad.

Attitudes of big employers to language competence of members of their staff vary. Some give special consideration to applicants with languages, in particular spoken skills, and may pay a language allowance. Others utilize the language capability of their staff without recognition. Yet others provide opportunities for members of staff to study and qualify.

6 Linguists in international organizations

The European Commission, the United Nations and the United Nations Educational, Scientific and Cultural Organization (UNESCO) are major employers of linguists. They require specialist linguists, that is translators and interpreters, and language competence in many of their administrative functions.

Recruitment is by competition, of which details are published in the media and through relevant professional bodies. Posts with these international bodies are heavily contested. For details write to them, but do not rely on a speedy response.

Interpreters, especially conference interpreters, have always been regarded as leading a glamorous jet-setting lifestyle and commanding high salaries. It is true that good conference interpreters can command high fees, but many of them are freelance and may, therefore, work only intermittently as interpreters. Posts and places on reserve lists of interpreters in international organizations are widely publicized and attract applicants from many parts of the world. Each advertised post is, therefore, heavily contested, often by bilingual speakers from different countries. Anyone interested in these posts should be aware that the vast majority of applicants will fall by the wayside. Applicants from the UK do not always have comparable competence in more than one other language. Inaccurate or incomplete applications and lack of attention to detail are often drawbacks for applicants from the UK.

The European Commission

The Commission's Joint Interpretation and Conference Service (known by its French acronym of SCIC) covers all European institutions except the European Parliament, but each of these institutions has in addition its own individual translation service.

The Translation Service uses the SYSTRAN machine, which can produce 2000 raw pages of translation per hour – but a final scan by the human eye requiring many more hours to complete is still necessary.

The European Commission has a continuous need for conference interpreters and is one of the largest employers of interpreters in the world. There is a growing demand for interpreters offering additional language combinations as other European countries join the EU.

Promotion can be quite swift, but although the rewards are great, so is the competition at the recruitment stage. Although most Commission staff are employed in Brussels, some work is in Luxembourg and elsewhere in Europe and the rest of the world. Traineeships are available for prospective administrators. The Traineeships Office is administered by the Education and Culture Directorate General (see Web site www.europa. eu.int/comm/stages).

Salaries

From the year 2000, salaries are paid only in Euros and are subject to exchange rate fluctuations. For graduates with little or no experience, the starting monthly salary is usually €3,850, and for graduates with at least two to three years' experience €4,350. Depending on the competition, these rates apply if candidates meet the standard requirement of competence in two or three EU languages in addition to their own.

The United Nations and UNESCO

The United Nations and UNESCO, its educational arm, are

amongst the world's largest employers of translators and inter-preters. They require language services in many, if not most of the world's languages. A major concern of UNESCO is the third world and this is reflected in their language requirements.

7

How to make your language(s) work for you in the short term

Language skills, especially oral skills, are a great asset socially or when travelling. They may help to provide temporary jobs and some earnings in the short term. As these jobs are not necessarily advertised as such, you may need to search for them and make the initial contact. Events, exhibitions and trade fairs that attract tourists or visitors from abroad as well as summer schools may be advertised locally or in your region. However, specialist linguist functions should not be undertaken unless you are qualified.

Explore your own language or ethnic group locally or regionally. There may be some temporary work requiring your language skills.

Seasonal work

Some work with languages is seasonal and may, therefore, provide short-term employment. This applies to recent school leavers or students waiting to go to college or university and to recent graduates waiting or looking for their first job. Many of these jobs require no special training.

Such jobs may provide a taste of work with languages and some earnings, even just for a few weeks. However, while any language skills may help to bridge the communications gap, job seekers should be aware of the dangers of using, for example, limited language skills for interpreting in a health or legal context. If you know your locality well, helping out as a local guide may be a possibility, especially during the tourist season.

TEFL

Private tuition and supervising children's homework can be done from home and provide some experience as a tutor. Helping in one of the many summer schools for EFL may provide a first insight into teaching EFL. The summer being a busy time of year for schools of English, finding such a job may be relatively easy.

You may like to combine study and short-term work by teaching English while studying for an ELT/TEFL qualification. This is sometimes possible for language graduates who, it is assumed, would be able to pick up some basic TEFL relatively quickly as they have had experience with learning languages themselves.

Mother tongue maintenance

There is a growing trend in support of mother tongue maintenance, especially for children and young people in the British education system whose mother tongue is not English. Usually such tuition takes place on Saturdays and is provided by native speakers. Some of this work is voluntary. It gives aspiring language tutors and young people with a command of the language an opportunity and the confidence to practise the language in a learning environment. Information of these initiatives may be available from local authorities and some local colleges.

The tourist trade

Jobs abroad might include work in the hotel, leisure and

catering business. Occasionally your language skills may secure a temporary summer job as a courier for one of the tour operators or as a receptionist or guide at international exhibitions. Local travel agents may need language skills on a temporary or permanent basis. International youth camps offer the opportunity of working with languages and enjoying outdoor life during the summer months.

Other opportunities

Working as an au pair abroad, usually for six to 12 months, should enable language students to improve their language before attending university or college, see something of the country and earn their keep. They are expected to work a specified number of hours a day, up to six days a week. Conditions should be agreed in advance, including pay and pocket money. Au pair jobs are now open to both sexes, although the employer may have a particular preference.

You may wish to spend a whole year abroad working as a foreign language assistant in a school there. This would provide a basic income. The school would have some responsibility for you, and help is usually available so that you can find your feet generally and secure accommodation. Other possibilities include the Voluntary Service Overseas (VSO) or work at international archaeological sites. Information is available from the British Council.

If you have IT skills, you may be able to combine these with your knowledge of a language by keying in foreign language texts, for example projects, extended essays or dissertations of language students at undergraduate or postgraduate level although they frequently also have IT skills. As these are required at particular times, usually spring and early summer, you need to make contact with your local college or university at the right time.

Also, colleges and universities frequently make their campus facilities available to summer schools of English. They may have casual requirements for English or other language speakers.

They also need administrative or clerical assistants. If you speak a European language, say Italian, an English summer school in your locality, for Italians, may welcome the fact that you can communicate with their students (frequently aged 14 to 16).

8 Getting in and getting on

1. Make a list of all your skills including languages and match it against the skills needed for the jobs in which you are interested. Are there any obvious gaps to fill (by evening classes, further study, work experience)?
2. Never miss an opportunity to improve and use your language skills: socially, travelling, reading, films or videos and clubs.
3. Languages could lead to temporary jobs in local businesses, summer schools, events, voluntary work, youth camps or vacation work. See your local press, job centre and local authority publications.
4. Scan job vacancy sections in the local, national and specialist press for jobs; contact job centres, professional bodies, chambers of commerce, local or national organizations. Ask the reference section of your local library for other sources of information.
5. Acquire word processing/IT skills, possibly in evening classes or a short course. Almost everybody needs them today.
6. Prepare a speculative letter of application (using skills set out under point 5). Select at least 10–15 companies/organizations (using the information from 4 above). Indicate your interest and skills rather than

the need to earn money. The more letters you send, the better chance you have.

7. Look for training schemes and mention in your letters (6 above) that you would consider a traineeship. Training schemes could be part of a college course.

8. Consider working abroad where they speak a language you know (even if just a little). Use the local reference library for sources of information, journals and papers. Use exchange schemes at college or the year abroad during your degree course to identify organizations abroad for work experience or a job.

9. Send speculative letters, possibly in their language, to 10-15 employers or organizations abroad.

10. Set up a database of useful organizations in the UK and abroad with contact names and full addresses, telephone numbers, etc. Constantly update and extend and select contacts when you send speculative letters. Follow up the contacts you made under 6. Also use Chapter 10 for further reading and for useful addresses.

11. Use your IT skills to search the Net. Many vacancies are advertised in this way by government departments, employers in general and professional bodies.

12. Make contact with social networks in your locality, based on your language. They exist throughout Britain and are usually excellent mutual support systems. Also explore town twinning arrangements.

9 Future prospects for careers with languages

1. To catch up with their trading partners abroad, UK companies are beginning to realize the urgent need to improve their language capability. As a result, in-company language training is a growth area and continuing education courses for languages are also well attended. The provision of such courses could be a growing market, too.
2. Growing acceptance of lifelong learning as an essential dimension of the job market facilitates the prospect of learning a language while in employment.
3. To assist British industry in meeting its language needs, the Department of Trade and Industry (DTI) has set up a language service for industry, the National Business Language Information Service (NatBLIS), which provides information on language training, and translation and interpreting services for British businesses.
4. As British companies set up subsidiaries abroad, in the European Union, the USA and East Asia for example, and foreign companies, eg Japanese, French or German, take over companies in the UK, the demand for language capability at all levels, including the shop floor, will continue to grow.
5. In the UK itself, the need to communicate with non-English speakers, immigrants, tourists and job seekers from abroad is ever growing as they may require access to justice, and to social and medical services on an equal basis.
6. As the European Union offers free movement of labour to all Europeans, jobs are increasingly open to applicants from

any of the EU member states. Those with high level skills in other languages stand the best chance of success regardless of their country of origin.

7. There are growing signs that companies who need to communicate in another language increasingly look for native speakers to represent them in local markets. Also, where language training is part of a British company's strategy, there is increasingly a marked preference for trainers who are native speakers of the language required.

8. There are similar trends in various other EU countries where native English speakers are usually in demand as language trainers for English as a foreign language and as translators into English.

9. Language skills may be required by international companies and consortia with interests abroad (banking, marketing), UK-based companies with an international marketing strategy and British companies with export markets abroad. The need to communicate in the required language is the same for all.

10. To be prepared for these communications needs, individual career seekers should make sure at the earliest stage (GCSE, A-levels) that another language (or languages) forms part of their initial skills package to ensure a maximum choice of jobs in the future.

11. As the demand for greater specialization and, therefore, for higher qualifications, grows there is also a growing demand for postgraduate qualifications, especially in interpreting and translation and in language skills combined with other subject areas such as engineering, marketing or law.

12. The realization is gaining ground that those who are able to use language skills, however acquired, in the workplace should be able to qualify and that they should do so on the basis of nationally recognized standards which, in particular, meet the employers' expectations. To put such standards in place the National Language Standards were created and a national framework of vocational qualifications (NVQs) with langugage units as required (see Chapter 10).

10 Study and career options: how to acquire language skills

According to the Nuffield Language Inquiry 2000 first destination surveys indicate that recent graduates with language qualifications have the lowest level of unemployment after medical graduates.

With technology-based teaching aids (audio, video, distance and computer aided language learning) study has never been easier. The current trend of a decreasing uptake of languages at GCSE and A-level at school does not continue into adult life and employment. An ever-increasing demand for language tuition at the Open University and in Adult and Continuing Education highlights the need for language capability. This is matched by a demand for language qualifications at all levels.

Nonetheless, school students should be encouraged to take up languages early as they stand a better chance at a later stage of achieving the much sought after higher levels of competence with relative ease. In any case, for many business or job related situations any language skills are valuable.

Employers in the UK, the EU and beyond increasingly recruit from a multinational and multilingual pool of applicants. However, frequently they also require proof that language competence has not just been 'picked up' during a stay abroad but has been assessed and certificated, unless the applicant is a native speaker of the language required by the employer.

The notion that spending time abroad means you learn to speak the language like the natives is very attractive but may sometimes be little more than wishful thinking. You may pick up some phrases as a survival kit but may not be able to create coherent sentences. Employers may not be impressed by such language skills alone, but require certificates as evidence that a job applicant successfully undertook structured learning, even at the lower levels.

Psycholinguistic studies indicate that motivation to learn a language is the best guarantee that effective learning will take place. Working for a qualification is a strong motivating factor. Therefore, in general terms, learning a language is usually most effective if it is structured and leads to a qualification, although spending time abroad where the language is spoken can be fun and creates the confidence to use the language more effectively. This in turn helps to motivate the learner.

The view that the best way to learn a language is by staying in the country where it is spoken is, therefore, only partially correct. Learning a language abroad is usually a fast process. You need an instant survival kit (numbers, asking the way, buying food, etc) but you are likely to pick up not much more than a few expressions unless you stay in the country for a considerable period of time. Classroom teaching provides the learner with structures, vocabulary and some idiom that can be used in many different contexts.

A combination of learning at home (classroom or self-access) and abroad offers the best way of learning some theory first and then trying out how to apply it in real life. Acquiring a foreign language using up-to-date multi-media learning aids can be enjoyable. It is also a long-term commitment, whether the language is acquired through tuition in Britain or when staying abroad in the country of the language.

First degree courses in modern languages

Why a degree course?
◆ To continue your interest in languages after school.

◆ To learn in a more adult environment.
◆ To meet a wider range of people.
◆ As a basis for your future career.

Which degree course?
◆ Does the course offer one, two or three languages?
◆ Is the study of languages combined with another subject?
◆ How much is taught in these languages, not in English?
◆ The year abroad – where and for how long?
◆ What reputation in language studies does the institution enjoy?
◆ How far from home?
◆ Where do your friends study?

Which career?
To consider this question is at least as important as knowing that you would like to study languages. It may affect much of your working life and is a major factor in choosing a particular degree course. Are you thinking of languages in:

◆ business
◆ the professions
◆ teaching, in schools, colleges, universities
◆ interpreting
◆ translation?

This book seeks to provide some of the answers.

Sources of information

As a wide range of language degree courses are on offer, you should consult the major specialist publications, using the above check list. In particular the *UCAS Handbook*, which is updated annually, and the *CRAC Degree Course Guides*, published separately according to language, sometimes combined with other subjects, provide full details.

Applied language studies degrees

Language is not a subject in itself but a means to access knowledge and culture and to communicate. Modern language degrees, therefore, tend to be based on integrated area study programmes which may include social studies, politics, economics or business studies usually relating to the country or countries concerned. These options may be taught in English or the other language. More tuition in the language may lead to a higher level of foreign language competence. A few language degree courses continue to offer literature as an option.

The year abroad

Modern language degree courses today may have a year (or more) abroad built into the course, which students spend in one or two countries to consolidate the language or languages they are studying. Students usually spend the year abroad at a university or college attending classes, often together with students of the host country. A few first degree courses include work experience abroad.

Choosing a language degree course involves decisions on the year abroad. Do you want to spend the year at a university or in work placement, in which country (eg Spain or Latin America, France or French-speaking Canada) and which options do you prefer? All these decisions have career implications.

The Honours element in first degree courses

Most modern language degree courses lead to the award of a BA Hons degree. The Honours element is as a rule clearly identifiable. If a course appears to be too demanding to individual students, they may have the choice of an ordinary BA degree by not taking the Honours element. However, a good Honours degree is likely to secure a higher salary later.

If languages are your main interest, you need to consider a modern languages degree course with one, two or three foreign languages. The second and in particular the third language may be studied from beginners level or post-GCSE.

In addition to the award of a BA degree in the UK, a few of these courses also lead to qualifications from the other country or countries, a point that needs careful consideration.

European studies degree courses

These courses tend to offer one language, possibly two. The level of language proficiency attained at the end of the course may well be lower than that of a modern languages degree course because European Studies degree courses tend to concentrate more on the study of politics and economics in Europe and of European institutions.

Careers implications of your degree course

Before choosing your degree course, you need to consider what career alternatives exist and how they appeal to you. You may wish to opt for one of the linguist professions for which a high level of language competence is a primary requirement, in particular translation, interpreting and language teaching. For these, a modern language degree plus a postgraduate qualification are the usual routes.

If you choose a combined course including a language, your postgraduate studies are unlikely to be in languages but in marketing, management or law, or an MBA course, sometimes including a language.

A note of caution: there is currently a strong trend amongst British universities to reduce drastically or close down altogether language departments which used to offer modern language degree courses. On the other hand, there is a steadily growing number of university degree courses in other subjects include the opportunity to study a language that in order to provide engineers, lawyers and other professionals with the skills to function in the EU or elsewhere in the global economy.

Financial aspects

This area is currently in such a state of flux that students are advised to clarify their own particular financial situation in advance. Information should be available from UCAS and from sixth-form careers advisers. Your course fees are as a rule paid by the local authority in whose area you live or lived just prior to your first term or semester at university. Make sure all financial aspects have been clarified in advance.

Higher National Diploma (HND) courses with languages

HND courses usually extend over two years' full-time study. Some offer a language as an option, in particular some HND courses in business studies, hospitality, leisure and tourism, hotel management and catering. Entrance requirements are one to two A-levels or two AS-levels plus GCSEs, but some courses have been oversubscribed in the past (in particular leisure and tourism) and may be highly selective in their students. These courses increasingly offer NVQs.

Information on HNDs and other vocational diplomas is available from Edexcel, the awarding body for these qualifications. The new Languages National Training Organization (LNTO) should be able to provide information on NVQs with language units. (Contact CILT for further information.)

Postgraduate and professional courses

Interpreters, translators and language teachers require a high level of language competence as a primary skill. Students who are especially interested in high level professional language skills may, therefore, opt for a career in interpreting or translation. They may wish to choose degree courses which include tuition for these skills, possibly through a translation and interpreting option in the final year. That does not as a rule qualify graduates to embark on a career as translator or interpreter. It enables them, however, to judge for themselves whether they are suited for these specialist areas and would enjoy such a career.

Training courses for interpreters and translators

Speaking two languages, however fluently, does not as such guarantee translation and interpreting skills. As a rule, these require training as well as initial professional experience. In today's age of specialization prospective translators and interpreters are likely to attend a one-year postgraduate course in translating and/or interpreting. These courses vary in some respects (linguistics, subject knowledge for technical translation) but include extensive practice and professional training in translation and/or interpreting.

During the past few years there has been a considerable increase in such courses in the UK. The Universities of Bath, Bradford, Kent, Salford, Surrey and Westminster have postgraduate courses in this field which are well known. UMIST, the University of Manchester Institute of Science and Technology, offers a postgraduate course in machine translation. New courses for translation have been set up by a growing number of other institutions.

Postgraduate courses in interpreting or translation vary in subjects and languages. You should check what is available at the time. (Consult the *CRAC Student's Guide to Graduate Studies in the UK*, which is updated annually.)

Some MA courses in translation studies deal with translation theory and do not necessarily offer translation practice in your particular language combination.

Postgraduate qualifications for interpreting and translation are popular with mature students who change careers in mid-life and with translators who feel the need to upgrade their credentials with a postgraduate qualification.

A number of universities and colleges in the UK and abroad offer part-time and short intensive courses leading to the Diploma in Translation of the Institute of Linguists (DipTrans IoL). This flexible course provision makes the qualification more accessible for people in work and is, therefore, popular with mature students and practising translators. It is pitched at a professional level and is comparable to the standard achieved in one-year postgraduate courses. (A list of courses in the UK and abroad is available from the Institute of Linguists. See also Chapter 11.)

The DipTrans IoL qualification was introduced to ensure standards throughout the profession, which is still unregulated in the UK. It very soon became a benchmark for standards expected of practising translators.

Training courses for public service interpreting

A new range of part-time courses has been developed at colleges and universities since the mid-1990s to provide much needed training for interpreters working for the public services. These courses lead to the Diploma in Public Service Interpreting (DPSI) of the Institute of Linguists. This qualification is unique in the UK and has national recognition. It was created to provide qualified interpreters for the police and courts and other legal agencies, local and central government departments, health care and for legal interpreting in Scotland.

These courses may be of varying length depending on the experience and needs of the participants. The courses cover the major Central and East Asian, European and some African languages. The demand for interpreting in the public services arises from the needs of immigrants, ethnic groups, refugees, foreign workers, students and tourists alike. (A list of courses, languages and options is available from the Institute of Linguists. See also Chapters 4 and 11.)

Secretarial linguist courses

Courses and qualifications for secretarial linguists or bilingual secretaries have been transformed by the far-reaching effects of information technology. Increasingly, managers and professionals use IT to conduct their own correspondence, making shorthand typing, audio typing and other secretarial skills in English and other languages to some extent redundant. Secretarial linguist posts now take up more time with scheduling itineraries for visits abroad and for visitors' staying in

Britain, providing language services and ad hoc interpreting. Some posts have changed to office management.

A range of diplomas and higher diplomas in administrative and secretarial procedures including IT are available as RSA qualifications, though the awarding body is now OCR, an amalgam of examination boards including the Royal Society of Arts. Optional college courses lead to these qualifications, but candidates may also enter on the basis of prior experience. As language competence is increasingly a desirable or essential skill in this area, candidates can combine any of these diplomas with one or more NVQ language units on a flexible basis to suit their skills and the employer's needs (see Chapter 11).

Other language courses

Languages can be learned from beginner to postgraduate levels. For professional purposes, other than interpreting, translating and teaching, even quite elementary skills can play an important role in developing business contacts abroad. A number of universities and colleges offer courses, part-time day or evening, which lead to the examinations of the Institute of Linguists.

In addition, a wide range of foreign language courses at all levels, but mainly for post-beginners, are available at local colleges and the continuing education departments of universities. At the lower levels, courses may lead to certificates from City and Guilds, the London Chamber of Commerce and Industry Examinations Board (LCCIEB) and the Royal Society of Arts (RSA) Examinations Board. (See also Chapter 11.)

In the main these courses offer the four major European languages, but courses for Arabic, Japanese, Portuguese, Russian and the Scandinavian languages are also available. They lead in particular to Institute of Linguists qualifications. Information is available from the examining bodies or your local college. Londoners may also wish to consult the publications *Floodlight* and *On Course*. For information on courses in any language at any level throughout Britain contact *Learndirect*, freephone 0800 100 900.

11 Language qualifications and levels of competence

An increasing percentage of people today are graduates. Employers who offer jobs for which command of a language is essential, may, therefore, look for degree-level competence. (For details see Chapter 9.) The language competence which degree holders may attain varies considerably. It may or may not coincide with employers' expectations, although there is an increasing willingness on the part of employers to encourage and support language training of their employees.

Recognition within the EU

Another variable factor is recognition of qualifications within the EU. As there is now free movement of labour within the EU, British graduates may seek employment anywhere within the Union. Graduates from other countries within the EU may also compete for such posts or they could take on jobs in the UK. However, within the EU mutual recognition of qualifications including degrees may be handled differently in different member states and for different professions. Some UK course providers, usually universities, have overcome this problem by offering joint courses with comparable institutions abroad. On successful completion of some of these courses, graduates may hold a BA (Hons) as well as a Diploma from a German university and/or the French Maîtrisse or a graduate qualification from Spain. Some universities offer franchises to enable institutions abroad to run UK validated courses.

There is also an increasing demand for 'portable' qualifications. This term covers qualifications from major awarding bodies in the UK that are widely known. Regardless of the extremely slow progress of formal recognition of qualifications within the EU by member states on a mutual basis, some of these qualifications are beginning to gain recognition within individual EU countries.

Qualifications of this kind are available from a number of external awarding bodies, in particular the Institute of Linguists, OCR Oxford Cambridge RSA, the London Chamber of Commerce Examinations Board (mainly for EL), Trinity College London and City and Guilds of London Institute.

The Institute of Linguists Educational Trust

The Institute of Linguists is an awarding body accredited by the Qualifications and Curriculum Authority. All its qualifications are being submitted for inclusion in the National Framework of Qualifications.

Of the major external language examining bodies only the Institute of Linguists offers qualifications for specialist linguists (interpreting and translation) at professional level.

The Institute of Linguists Educational Trust has been offering language qualifications for many decades. They range from post-A-level standard to postgraduate levels. For professional purposes, the Institute's Educational Trust offers a range of diploma and intermediate diploma and certificate qualifications:

- ◆ Diploma in Translation
- ◆ Diploma in Public Service Interpreting
- ◆ Bilingual Skills Certificate
- ◆ Diploma in English for International Communication
- ◆ Diploma in Languages for International Communication
- ◆ Intermediate Diploma in Languages for International Communication
- ◆ Final diploma in English and Chinese

The Institute's diploma qualifications test language skills at degree equivalent level or specific skills at professional level. The intermediate diploma qualifications are at a somewhat lower level and holders tend to acquire the full diploma qualification at a subsequent stage.

No prior formal qualifications are required for any of these examinations, although they are of a very high standard. They offer an excellent opportunity to qualify as a linguist and join the Institute of Linguists as a professional member. This opportunity is also taken up by holders of other professional and academic qualifications including lawyers, accountants and engineers with a high level of language skills. Others who have language skills from their family or living abroad can go on improving their language skills and take language examinations at a lower level before qualifying as diploma holders.

Diploma in Translation

The Diploma in Translation (DipTrans IoL) has become a benchmark qualification for professional linguists entering the translator profession. It requires a high level of translation skills, good mother tongue written skills and detailed cultural knowledge of the country or countries concerned. The Diploma in Translation is available in up to 45 language combinations with English and tests reading, writing and translation skills. It covers the specialist areas of science, technology, business and the humanities as well as literature. It is much sought after by translation companies and employers who require the services of freelance or staff translators and is gaining increasing recognition in other EU countries.

When this qualification was first introduced in 1989, about one third of candidates were already working as translators who wanted to for-malize their status on the basis of the DipTrans IoL qualification. This has helped to eliminate unqualified practitioners and thereby improve standards nationally in the UK.

Diploma in Public Service Interpreting

The Diploma in Public Service Interpreting (DPSI) was created in 1994. Together with an earlier Institute of Linguists qualification, the Certificate in Community Interpreting, the DPSI is the only nationally recognized qualification for interpreting for police and courts and other legal agencies, in health care and local government including housing and education and the benefits agencies. The diploma in these various options is available in over 40 African, Asian, European and East Asian languages. It tests simultaneous whispering and ad hoc interpreting, sight translation and basic translation from and into English.

The DPSI caters for English and non-English native speakers who may subsequently join the National Register of Public Service Interpreters. Employers of DPSI holders are in the main public service providers, police and courts and local or central government agencies. (See also Chapter 3.)

Bilingual Skills Certificate

The Bilingual Skills Certificate (BSC) is a pre-professional qualification frequently taken by public service workers who need to work in English and the language of their non-English speaking clients in housing, education or the health service. They may hold posts as bilingual public service workers, nurses or social workers. The benefits agencies are major employers of such bilingual workers. The BSC is also a preparatory examination for the DPSI.

Examinations in International Communication: Diploma and Advanced level

In vocational terms, the Examinations in International Communication (ELIC) Diploma is in particular sought after by language teachers as it may be recognized as a degree equivalent qualification for employment and also as entrance qualification for further study or research.

Diploma in English for International Communications

In level and status this qualification is comparable to the ELIC Diploma. It tests all four language skills in English at degree equivalent level.

Intermediate ELIC Diploma

The Intermediate Diploma is a general practical language qualification at basic professional level. Holders may also use it as a stepping stone for one of the diploma qualifications. It is popular with people whose employment requires increasingly higher language competence.

Final Diploma in English and Chinese

This qualification was created as a vocational equivalent to a degree for Chinese and English speakers in Hong Kong. In Australia it has recognition as a basic professional qualification. Increasingly the qualification is also taken in the UK by Chinese native speakers.

Other vocational language certificates

In addition, the Institute of Linguists offers language tests from post-beginners upwards through its subsidiary, Language Services Ltd. The Institute of Linguists offers tailor-made examinations in a very wide range of languages including most major and less commonly taught European languages, languages of the Indian subcontinent, East Asian and African languages and rare languages spoken in the community.

National Language Standards (NLS)

There are many people for whom the acquisition of language skills in the workplace becomes desirable or even essential as the market situation changes or their own role develops in the business, industry or service in which they are employed. Today this need is fully recognized. It is now possible for employees to obtain a nationally recognized qualification other than through the traditional channels. Furthermore, this qualification, awarded through attainment of the NLS, is designed to meet workplace requirements.

The NLS units are more flexible in use than most other NVQ units in that they can be awarded individually, either as part of, and enhancing, an NVQ as 'optional' or 'additional' units or separately, as 'free-standing' units. They are not linked in level to the occupational NVQ.

As with all NVQs, the NLS are assessed as units, each covering one of the four skills of listening, speaking, reading and writing at one of five levels from basic to professional linguist competence.

For instance, a practising engineer with NVQ at level 4 in occupational competence could choose to be trained or assessed in Spanish listening and speaking at NLS level 2. This might arise from an increasing export commitment or the need to liaise with a Spanish parent company. At this level the engineer would not be expected to negotiate at a high managerial or technical level in the language but recognizes the benefit to working relationships in being able to conduct informal work and social interactions in Spanish.

When evidence of competence has been produced, either in the work setting or through simulation, the candidate is accredited with the relevant units which may be combined with the NVQ certificate in applying for a future post in which the language qualification is seen as an advantage.

Another employee might seek an equally valid qualification through different units. His or her prevalent use of a foreign language at work might be in reading and writing only, for example in being able to summarize the context of incoming promotional literature or respond to correspondence in the foreign language. Here again, the achievement of the appropriate units earns a qualification in its own right.

This is, very broadly, how the NLS levels correspond to traditional qualifications:

NLS level
5 Good honours degree + substantial experience in using language in a high-level work context, eg negotiation at strategy/policy level, sensitive or highly technical dialogue, correspondence or report writing
4 Good honours degree, able to work independently in the language
3 Good A-level pass, able to work alongside foreign speaking colleague
2 Good GCSE pass, able to work alongside foreign speaking colleague
1 Lower GCSE pass (reasonably accurate but within a very limited range of context, vocabulary and structure)

The NLS are applicable to the assessment in a vocational context of any language foreign to the learner, eg to EFL, to languages spoken in the community such as Urdu and to 'heritage' languages such as Gaelic. Although they have been designed to address business and industrial needs, they respect the fact that a high proportion of language used at work may be 'generic' – applicable to most situations in life – especially at the lower levels. Even where, as at level 5, the candidate must be able to deal with highly specialized topics, it is not likely that the technical component of the required language will exceed five to ten per cent of vocabulary and idioms used.

Assessment is not by examination, but by judging evidence compiled by the candidate in a 'portfolio' against the criteria of the NLS. This frees the assessment process from the constraints of the calendar by allowing candidates to work towards the desired qualification within whatever timescale their work requirements may demand.

In 1997 the National Council for Vocational Qualifications was replaced by the Qualifications and Curriculum Authority (QCA), which has the same responsibilities in this field.

ELT qualifications

There is a worldwide demand for English language teaching. Whether or not such teachers are native English speakers, they are as a rule expected to hold an ELT qualification. Such qualifications are awarded by a number of external examining bodies, especially the Royal Society of Arts (RSA) jointly with the University of Cambridge Local Examinations Syndicate (UCLES) as well as Trinity College London. They offer ELT qualifications at various levels.

These qualifications are recognized by the British Council.

The RSA/UCLES Certificates and Diplomas

The Cambridge RSA qualifications for ELT are available at two levels. The certificates at initial level are known as CELTA and, for overseas teachers, COTE.

The CELTA qualification requires as a minimum a one-month intensive training course or about four months part-time course attendance. Admission is usually for English native or near native speakers with at least three GCSEs and two A-levels or at the discretion of the course provider. Minimum age is 20, no prior teaching experience is required. The COTE qualification is an early in-service training course for practising teachers who have relevant classroom experience with children or adults. For information on centres worldwide contact UCLES RSA.

The DELTA qualification (Diploma in English Language Teaching for Adults) is for graduates and qualified teachers with a minimum of two years teaching experience. Candidates must be native or near native speakers of English. Full-time courses normally take three to four months and part-time courses eight to nine months. In addition, 150 hours of study and research are part of the course.

CILTS: The Cambridge RSA also provide integrated English language teaching schemes from certificate to diploma levels (known as CILTS) covering teaching of children and adults in Britain and worldwide.

Trinity College London

Trinity College London offers similar qualifications. The Certificate in Teaching English to Speakers of Other Languages (TESOL) is designed for those with little or no experience in ELT. Trainees must follow an approved course. Course providers set their own entrance requirements based on a good standard of general education. In some cases, graduate or equivalent entrance qualifications are required. Minimum entrance age is 20 years.

The OCR Examinations Board (Oxford Cambridge RSA)

This is a large examinations board for a wide range of subjects. The language examinations concentrate on the major European languages and languages as a whole represent only a minor part of the range of subjects available.

OCR also provides schemes that enable candidates to obtain language units within the NVQ framework. A number of these units may form part of other NVQs, in particular in the field of business and also in catering. Full details are available from OCR.

The London Chamber of Commerce and Industry Examinations Board (LCCIEB)

The LCCIEB examines a very wide range of subjects including foreign language examinations. Foreign Languages at Work (FLAW) tests oral/aural skills only.

In addition, business English is offered by the LCCI.

In 2001 the LCCIEB Examinations Board launched a new range of modern languages examinations.

City and Guilds of London Institute

This is another large examinations board offering a variety of subject examinations and certificates of which languages are only a minor part. French, German, Italian and Spanish are offered in the main at the lower levels.

12 Useful addresses

Careers

For more details see Chapter 13.

Association of Graduate Careers Advisory Services (AGCAS)
http://www.agcas.csu.ac.uk

Association of Graduate Careers Services in Ireland (AGCSI), Careers Service, Trinity College, East Chapel, Dublin 2, Republic of Ireland; 00 3531 608 1721

Civil Service

Recruitment and Assessment Services for the Civil Service (CAPITA), Innovation Court, New Street, Basingstoke, Hampshire RG21 7JB; 01256 383780
http://www.capitaras.co.uk

Government Communications Headquarters (GCHQ), Government Communications Headquarters, Priors Road, Cheltenham, Glos GL52 5AJ; 01242 221491

Joint Technical Language Services (see GCHQ)

Diplomatic Service

Foreign and Commonwealth Office, Recruitment Section, Personnel Policy Department, 3 Central Buildings, Matthew Parker Street, London SW1H 9NL; 0207 270 1500

Educational

The British Council, 10 Spring Gardens, London SW1A 2BN; 0207 930 8466

The British Council, Education Counselling Service, Medlock Street, Manchester M15 4AA; 0161 957 7000

Centre for Information on Language Teaching and Research (CILT), 20 Bedfordbury, London WC2N 4LB; 0207 379 5101

Languages National Training Organization, address as for CILT, http://www.languagesnto.org.uk

Department for Education and Skills, Sanctuary Buildings, Great Smith Street, London SW1P 3BT; 0870 000 2288 http://www.dfes.gov.uk

Examining bodies

CACDP (Council for the Advancement of Communication with Deaf People) (British Sign Language interpreting), Durham University Science Park, Block 4, Stockton Road, Durham DH1 3UZ; 0191 383 1155

City and Guilds of London Institute, Giltspur Street, London EC1A 9DD; 0207 413 8400

Edexcel Stewart House, 32 Russell Square, London WC1B 5DN; 0207 413 8400

The Institute of Linguists Educational Trust, Saxon House, 48 Southwark Street, London SE1 1UN; 0207 940 3100

OCR Oxford Cambridge and RSA, 1 Hills Road, Cambridge CB1 2EU; 01223 552 552
http://www.ocr.org.uk

Qualifications and Curriculum Authority (QCA), 83 Piccadilly, London W1J 8QA; 0207 509 5555

Trinity College London, 89 Albert Embankment, London SE1 7TR; 0207 820 6100

For LCCI and LCCIEB see next section

Export, marketing and sales, industry and commerce

The Chartered Institute of Marketing, Moor Hall, Cookham, Nr Maidenhead, Berkshire SL6 9QH; 01628 427500

The Industrial Society, 48 Bryanston Square, London W1H 7EA; 0207 262 2401

The Institute of Exports, Export House, Minerva Business Park, Lynch Wood, Peterborough PE2 6FT; 01733 404 400

The London Chamber of Commerce and Industry, Athena House, 112 Station Road, Sidcup, Kent DA15 7BJ; 0208 302 0261

Finance and banking

Institute of Financial Services, 90 Bishopsgate, London EC2N 4AS; 0207 444 7111

Hospitality, leisure and tourism

British Airways Recruitment, PO Box 59, Hounslow, Middlesex TW5 9QX; 0870 608 0747
http://www.britishairwaysjobs.com

The Hotel, Catering and International Management Association (HCIMA), 191 Trinity Road, London SW17 7HN; 0208 772 7400

The Institute of Leisure and Amenity Management (ILAM), ILAM House, Lower Basildon, Nr Reading, Berks RG8 9NE; 01491 874800

The Institute of Sport and Recreation Management, Gifford House, 36–38 Sherrad Street, Melton Mowbray, Leics LE13 1XJ; 01664 565531

London Tourist Board and Convention Bureau, 1 Warwick Road, London SW1E 5ER; 0207 932 2000

The Tourist Guiding Foundation, Lloyds Court, Goodman's Yard, London E1 8AT; Fax: 0207 953 1257

International organizations

Commission of the European Communities, Rue de la Loi 200, B-1049 Brussels, Belgium

The European Commission, UK Office, 8 Storey's Gate, London SW1P 3AT; 0207 973 1992
http://www.cec.org.uk

United Nations Information Centre, 21st Floor, Millbank Tower, Millbank, London SW1P 4QH; 0207 630 1981

UNESCO, 7 Place de Fontenoy, 75352 Paris, France

Insurance

The Chartered Insurance Institute, London E18 2JP; 0208 989 8464

Journalism and media

BBC Recruitment, Henry Wood House, 3 and 6 Langham Place, London W1A 1AA; 0208 743 8000

Institute of Journalists, 2 Dock Offices, Surrey Quays Road, London SE16 2XU; 0207 252 1187

The Newspaper Society, Training Department, Bloomsbury House, Bloomsbury Square, 74-77 Great Russell Street, London WC1B 3DA; 0207 636 7014

Book publishing: contact individual publishing houses

Language teachers

Association of Language Learning (ALL), 150 Railway Terrace, Rugby CV21 3HN; 01788 546443
http://www.all-languages.org.uk

Department for Education and Skills, Sanctuary Buildings, Great Smith Street, London SW1P 3BT; 0845 6000
http://www.dfes.gov.uk

General Teaching Council for Scotland Advisory Service on Entry to Teaching in Scotland, 5 Royal Terrace, Edinburgh EH7 5AF; 0131 556 0072

Teachers Training Agency, Portland House, Stag Place, London SW1E 5TT; 0207 925 3700
http://www.canteach.gov.uk

Teaching information helpline: 0845 56991

Legal

The Law Society, 113 Chancery Lane, London WC2A 1PL
http://www.lawsociety.org.uk

Law Society of Scotland, Law Society's Hall, 26 Drumsheugh Gardens, Edinburgh EH3 7YR; 0131 226 7411

Law Society of Northern Ireland, Law Society House, 98 Victoria Street, Belfast BT1 3JZ; 02890 231 614

Law Society of Ireland, Dublin, Republic of Ireland; 00 353 1671 4800

Librarianship and information science

Association for Information Management (ASLIB), Information House, 20-24 Old Street, London, EC1V 9AP; 0207 903 0000

The Institute of Information Scientists, London; 0207 619 0624

The Library Association; London; 0207 255 0500

Media – see Journalism
Patent agents and examiners

The Chartered Institute of Patent Agents, Staple Inn Buildings, High Holborn, London WC1V 7PZ; 0207 405 9450
http://www.cipa.org.uk

European Patent Office, Erhardstrasse 27, D-80331 Munich, Germany; 00 49 89 23990

The Patent Office, Concept House, Cardiff Road, Newport, Gwent NP10 8QQ; 01633 814000

Professional bodies for linguists

Association Internationale des Interprètes de Conference (AIIC), 10 Avenue de Sécheron, CH-1202 Geneva, Switzerland; 00 41 22 7313323
http://www.aiic.net

Institute of Linguists, Saxon House, 48 Southwark Street, London SE1 1UN; 0207 940 3100
http://www.iol.org.uk

Institute of Translation and Interpreting (ITI), Exchange House, 494 Midsummer Boulevard, Central Milton Keynes; 01908 255 905
http://www.iti.org.uk

Translators Association (TA), 84 Drayton Gardens, London SW10 9SB; 0207 373 6642

Teaching English as a Foreign Language

Association of Recognized English Language Services (ARELS), 56 Buckingham Gate, London SW1E 6AG; 0207 802 9200

The British Council, English Language Information Section, Medlock Street, Manchester M15 4AA; 0161 957 7141

OCR Oxford Cambridge RSA (see examining bodies)

Trinity College London (see examining bodies)

Working abroad

British Council (addresses above, under Educational)

Voluntary Service Overseas (VSO), 317 Putney Bridge Road, London SW15 2PN; 0208 780 7200

13 Sources of information on careers with languages

Careers information is vital. It should be impartial and up-to-date. It is important in schools as the choice of some GCSEs and A-levels should be based on inclination and talent as well as on career considerations. Schools and colleges provide careers guidance, in particular for the sixth form. Careers information is again vital when leaving school and considering work or a course of study, a degree or HND course or other vocational training. Careers information is also essential for anyone seeking a career change at a later stage.

Careers advice

During their post-A-level studies, students are advised to establish contact with the careers advisers among the academic or training staff and to do so well before the start of the final year of the course.

Careers advice is also available from local authority job centres and local authority careers and equal opportunity sections. Excellent advice and guidance may be obtained in individual interviews. Some Citizens Advice Bureaux also provide careers information, and the reference section of your local library should be able to point out further sources of information.

Careers advisers may assist in a number of ways. They may be able to indicate possible avenues to explore if you are uncertain as to what you might like to do in the future. They may be able to help you if you lack the confidence or knowledge to think positively about a worthwhile future career. Or you may know what you would like to take up but have doubts about your suitability or competence. Job seekers may have only a vague goal like 'something to do with the environment' and only a few are likely to see a careers adviser with specific questions about a clearly defined career.

Many career seekers are likely to start off without a clear goal ahead of them, but as they collect more and more information the possibilities for a future career become clearer. This process of inquiry itself may be instrumental in removing uncertainties and enable the career seeker to focus more precisely on a particular occupational area and eventually outline a possible career path. Establishing a good relationship with the careers advisers is useful as you should expect to talk to them not just once but on a number of occasions so that you may get all or most of your concerns explored and questions clarified.

It is useful to attend careers talks and consult careers literature at any stage. They can act as a curtain raiser, give you some initial ideas or answer specific questions. Career choices are important decisions that may affect your future. Take time to make them with knowledge and care.

Changes are always possible

Always remember, nothing is cast in stone, changes at later stages are possible and often beneficial. Also remember that virtually everything you ever learned will be useful at a later stage, even if you change your course of study or your chosen career. Many people today change careers more than once and well into mid-life and are even more likely to do so in the future. Indeed, flexibility and change are likely to be features of most future career patterns. This applies in particular to jobs with languages because languages can be a passport to many different jobs in the British Isles and beyond.

Also, whether or not you like the prospect at this stage, there are ever increasing opportunities to qualify further at a later stage or retrain altogether or work abroad. The times when a career was a choice for life are well and truly gone, opening ever changing, interesting and challenging prospects for those who are prepared to search, train and try.

Useful publications

As careers opportunities change with the times, careers literature tends to be updated frequently. You need to ensure, therefore, that you always consult the latest edition. Also consult relevant Web sites.

For careers with languages the following may be useful:

1. Information dealing with study opportunities after leaving school.
2. Careers literature which sets out the range of career possibilities for those who have particular language qualifications or skills or who are currently acquiring them.
3. Information on working with languages abroad. As many of these publications are updated regularly, always consult the latest edition.

1. For studying languages the most important publications covering courses are:

◆ *UCAS Handbook and UCAS Big Guide*, published annually by UCAS (Fulton House, Jessop Avenue, Cheltenham, Glos GL50 3SH; Tel: 01242 222444) for complete information on first degree courses available in the UK (always consult the latest edition).
◆ *CRAC Degree Course Guides*, Hobsons Publishing (for various disciplines).
◆ *CRAC Directory of Higher Education*, Hobsons Publishing (covering all disciplines).
◆ *Getting into languages*, Trotman & Co Ltd, a useful factual account of what is involved in studying languages, concen-

trating on first degrees but also covering other courses with languages.

2. Careers information and literature:

Careers information is now available to a great extent on the Internet. Some employers publicise their vacancies on their Web sites expecting interested job seekers to consult them. Some Web site addresses are included in the chapter to which they refer while some of the most important Web site addresses and publications for careers with languages are listed here. Please note that Web site addresses are sometimes subject to change:

◆ *The Association of Graduate Careers Advisory Services AGCAS* at http://www.agcas.csu.ac.uk. There are associated Web sites for AGCAS Scotland and Ireland.
◆ *CILT, the Centre for Information on Language Teaching and Research,* offers professional advice for new and established language taechers at http://www.cilt.org.uk.
◆ *ELT Guide* for ELT and TEFL training and jobseekers at http://www.elgazette.co.eltguide.html
◆ *LNTO, the Languages National Training Organization;* information on careers success with languages at http://www. languagesnto.org.uk/careers/careersmenu.htm
◆ *LNTO:* A number of regional surveys of language needs and language capability in the UK were carried out for LNTO by Stephen Hagen. Executive summaries available from LNTO at http://www.languagesnto.org.uk/regional/ regionalmenu.html
◆ *Prospects,* the official publishers of HE careers guidance with hundreds of graduate jobs and over 15,500 postgraduate courses, research places and careers at http://www. prospects.csu.ac.uk

See also the following publications:
◆ *CILT Guide to Languages and Careers: How to continue your languages into further and higher education (1999).*
◆ *Graduates and their Careers,* from the Association of Graduate Careers Services in Ireland.

◆ *The Penguin Careers Guide* covers a wide range of career opportunities and includes a section on languages and linguists.
◆ *Careers using Languages*, Kogan Page, 2002, is an in-depth guide to careers for linguists including advice on training and qualifications.

3. Working with languages abroad:
The British Council has information on English language teaching worldwide and on placements for English language assistants abroad.

The European Commission has published a number of booklets on living and working in another country available from the Commission's UK Office.

In 2001 the European Commission reported on the 'Eurobarometer', a pan-European survey of language skills. See http://www.europe.en.int/comm/edcuation/languages.html

The *Culture Shock* series of publications provides useful information on how to take account of cultural differences.

Professional bodies

Professional bodies represent a major source of information for career seekers. They are usually well informed and up-to-date. But bear in mind:

◆ their prime function is to serve their profession and members rather than the general public
◆ their information may be specialized rather than general
◆ they are not careers advisers
◆ the time they can give to career inquiries may be limited
◆ they may be on the look-out for new members

The professional bodies for linguists each make a different contribution to the linguist profession and the careers advice you may receive from any one of them may vary accordingly.

The Institute of Linguists

This is by far the largest of the professional bodies in the field. It was established in 1910 to help improve language capability in the UK, in particular industry and commerce. It is a professional body of highly qualified linguists worldwide. It has membership divisions for translators, interpreters, language teachers and academics, and linguists in industry and commerce. There are regional societies for members in the UK and abroad. The Institute of Linguists Educational Trust provides language examinations and, together with the Institute's Language Services Ltd, is reputed to have the largest network of language examiners in the British Isles at the higher levels.

The Institute of Linguists operates the National Register of Public Service Interpreters which covers professional interpreting for the legal agencies, health care and local government and offers earnings opportunities for qualified interpreters in many languages spoken in the community.

Because of its broad base, the Institute of Linguists can provide wide ranging careers information on all aspects of careers for linguists including interpreting, translating, teaching and many others. Information, including specialist careers literature, is available from the Publicity and Membership department. See www.iol.org.uk

The Institute of Translation and Interpreting

This was established in 1986 as a breakaway group from the Institute of Linguists. It has its own terms of reference, namely to represent the interests of translators and interpreters, and has its own code of conduct. Members can opt to join regional, language or subject networks.

Inquirers seeking information on careers are likely to be advised specifically on careers for interpreters and translators. There is a range of publications for sale. See www.iti.org.uk

The Translators Association

This is a small select body of translators and is closely associated with the Society of Authors. The main criterion for admission to the TA is evidence of published translations. Originally such translations were exclusively of a literary nature, although more recently other published translations are taken into consideration. Careers information is likely to have little general application unless a budding translator intends to translate primarily for publication.

The Association of Police and Court Interpreters

This is a specialist body that caters for court and police interpreters who represent a section of the interpreters profession. As the police and courts require a very wide range of languages, the APCI may be interested in linguists competent in the more uncommon languages. Its members may also qualify to join the National Register of Public Service Interpreters.

Association Internationale des Interprètes de Conference (AIIC)

This is the international association of conference interpreters, a relatively small band of highly qualified interpreters, as conference interpreting is regarded as the most specialized and skilful form of interpreting. The British Isles have their own AIIC representatives.

The Association of Translators and Interpreters (Ireland)

This body represents the interests of interpreters and translators in the Republic of Ireland.

Index